D0406081

DISCOVER *your* SALES STRENGTHS

OTHER BESTSELLING BOOKS FROM THE GALLUP ORGANIZATION

FOLLOW THIS PATH:
How the World's Greatest Organizations Drive Growth
by Unleashing Human Potential
by Curt Coffman and Gabriel Gonzalez-Molina, Ph.D.

NOW, DISCOVER YOUR STRENGTHS
by Marcus Buckingham and Donald O. Clifton, Ph.D.

FIRST, BREAK ALL THE RULES:
What the World's Greatest Managers Do Differently
by Marcus Buckingham and Curt Coffman

DISCOVER *your* SALES STRENGTHS

HOW THE WORLD'S GREATEST SALESPEOPLE DEVELOP WINNING CAREERS

BENSON SMITH & TONY RUTIGLIANO

WARNER
BUSINESS
BOOKS™

Published by Warner Books

An AOL Time Warner Company

Copyright © 2003 by The Gallup Organization
All rights reserved.

 Warner Business Books are published by Warner Books, Inc.,
1271 Avenue of the Americas, New York, NY 10020.

Visit our Web site at www.twbookmark.com.

 An AOL Time Warner Company

The Warner Business Books logo is a trademark of Warner Books, Inc.

Printed in the United States of America
First Printing: February 2003
10 9   8   7

The Library of Congress Cataloging-in-Publication Data

Smith, Benson.
    Discover your sales strengths : how the world's greatest salespeople develop
winning careers / Benson Smith & Tony Rutigliano.
        p. cm.
    ISBN 0-446-53047-6
    1. Selling. 2. Sales management. 3. Sales personnel—Vocational guidance. I.
Rutigliano, Tony. II. Title.

HF5438.25 .S625 2003
658.85—dc21   2002074092

Book design by Giorgetta Bell McRee

ACKNOWLEDGMENTS

Many individuals helped turn this book into a reality. We want to express our gratitude.

Thanks to Donald O. Clifton, Ph.D., for his pioneering work that led us to much of our understanding about sales forces and great salespeople. Throughout the whole process of writing this book we have appreciated and benefited from the constant encouragement, support, and vision from Jim Clifton, Larry Emond, and Paul Witherby. We also want to thank Mick Zangari, Ph.D., for decades of research and his numerous contributions to this text. Barb Sanford and Geoff Brewer made invaluable editorial comments. Marcus Buckingham and Curt Coffman contributed many key concepts from their earlier publications.

A host of dedicated Gallup readers made significant improvements to the text and include Brian Brim, Guido DeKoning, John Fleming, Alec Gallup, Gabriel Gonzalez-Molina, Jim Harter, Sharon Lutz, Bill McEwen, Danielle Newman, Rachel Penrod, Evan Perkins, Paul Petters, Tom Rath, Julie Ray, Mark Stiemann, Rosemary Travis, and Kryste Wiedenfeld. Thanks also to Cinda Hicks for all her help in a thousand different ways.

Thanks also go to the folks at Warner Books and specifically our editor, Rick Wolff, for his enthusiastic support, trust, and superb advice.

Special thanks to our wives and families for putting up with us during this process. For Benson, that's Melissa, Jason, Cameron, Jordan, and Hayden Smith. For Tony, that's Karen, Meghan, and Eugene.

CONTENTS

CHAPTER 1

The Wizard's Instructions

There are no jobs with a future, only people with a future.

A few years ago we were making our way down Bourbon Street in the New Orleans French Quarter. We had finished our meetings for the day and were in search of a cold beverage. It was late afternoon, and the street was already filling up with visitors. As we stopped at a corner, two boys about ten years of age came up and began studying our shoes intently. Just as we started to move along, one of the boys held out his hand and said, "Wait—I bet you a dollar I can tell you where you got them shoes."

We thought there was no real chance he could do this since we were from out of town. It would be a million-to-one shot for him to guess where we had bought our shoes, and even greater odds to guess for both of us because we were from different cities. "Are you going to tell us just the city or the store name?" we asked. He stared a bit more at our shoes and held out his own bet to his friend (more like his accomplice), who had somehow become the official money holder for this wager. He said, "I will tell you exactly, and I mean *exactly*, where you got them." With that, we both handed over our dollars.

After a few seconds the boy looked up at us and said, "Now, remember, I didn't say I was gonna tell you where you bought those shoes. I said I was gonna tell you exactly where you got 'em. Right now, you got your shoes on your feet on Bourbon Street."

With that, they both turned and ran down the street with our money. It wasn't until that moment—as our eyes were following them through the crowd—that we saw the wizard. He was heading our way down Bourbon Street. He was easy to spot. Dressed in a flowing purple costume with a peaked, purple wizard hat, he pulled a wishing well behind him. Even in the French Quarter, he looked a little bizarre. As he drew closer, we could see a sign on his well that read WISHES OF ALL KINDS GRANTED.

Perhaps we had our own signs painted on our foreheads that said TOURISTS: EASY MARKS, because he stopped right next to us. Intrigued by his appearance, we asked what the going rate for a wish was these days. He eyed us up and down and, taking in our suits, asked, "Is this a business wish or a personal wish?" "Business," we replied. "Well," he said, "those are a bit more complicated. Personal wishes are only a dollar, but business wishes are three dollars. Of course, with a business wish, you get a lot more for your money!"

Sure you do, we thought, but what the heck, this still had to be a better deal than spending a dollar each just to be told our shoes were on our feet, so we handed over three dollars. At that point he looked at us and said, "That's three dollars apiece." So, we coughed up another three dollars, and the wizard went to work.

He began waving his hands slowly in the air and speaking in a raspy wizard's voice. He instructed us to imagine clearly the wishes we had in mind. Then he asked us to visualize what would happen when our wishes were fulfilled. As we concentrated on this, he continued his incantation.

When he was satisfied we had clearly visualized our wishes, he said, "Now, think of all the gifts you have. Think about your physical gifts, your mental gifts, and your spiritual gifts. Think about all the different abilities and capabilities you have." He let us think for a moment as he continued his spell. Then, after a moment, he asked if we had those gifts clearly in mind. We both answered yes. He continued, "Think especially of those gifts and capabilities that would be useful in making your wish come true." And so we thought about which of our strengths might help us, and exactly how we would use them.

By this time a small crowd had gathered. This inspired the wizard to become even more dramatic. His demeanor became more mystical, his arm-waving more pronounced, and his voice even raspier. For six bucks we had our own Harry Potter Wizard on Bourbon Street. Then he said, "Now, I want you to think of all the people who might be able to help you make your wish come true. Not only people you know, but people you might meet who could help you. Think about what you would ask them to do and why they might want to help you." So, we thought of all the people who might help us to make our wishes come true.

While we were thinking about this, he threw flash paper into the air, which burst into flames. (Flambé of all kinds is popular in New Orleans.) The crowd was spellbound. Then, he asked us to close our eyes and think of the very first thing we could do to make our wishes come true. As we did this, he handed each of us a small card. "When you have the first step clearly in mind," he said, "open your eyes and read the card."

In a few minutes we opened our eyes. The wizard was already on his way with his wishing well in tow. The crowd had dissipated except for a few stragglers curious about what the cards said. We read the cards, looked at each other, and nodded our heads in agreement.

Many Wizards

Take away the flash paper, the purple costume, the raspy voice, and what do you have? Well, for one thing, you have a funny-looking man with a wishing well and six dollars of our money! Is this wizard's advice any good, or is it as worthless as being told your shoes are on your own feet? We were more than a little skeptical because over the years we have run into many self-proclaimed wizards, especially when it comes to advice about improved sales performance, a subject of keen interest to us.

More than forty years ago, our researchers became curious about why some people perform their roles so much better than others do. What was different about the very best teachers, managers, or leaders? Although we were interested in all these professions, and eventually studied them, we began our research into job performance by studying sales. This is because, of all careers, sales has the most quantifiable results—ultimately, the numbers tell the most important story of sales performance. Gallup focused primarily on salespeople who were consistently in the top 25 percent of their companies' sales forces. We found that the best performers sold four to ten times as much as average performers. These performers were not just incrementally better . . . they were *a lot* better. Customers not only bought more from them, but those same customers did it again and again. These top salespeople produced business with better margins. They tended to stay at their respective companies longer and developed more loyal relationships with their customers. We wanted to know what, if anything, is so special about such performers and why they are able to achieve so much more than their average counterparts.

Over the years we have interviewed more than 250,000 salespeople, more than one million customers, and 80,000 managers. This research produced some surprising conclusions—conclusions that refute many popularly held conceptions about sales excellence.

Dead Wrong

Yes, many "wizards" have written about exceptional sales performance. These books are sometimes big sellers. Just like the newest diet books, they promise spectacular results. But lasting improvement from either kind of book is hard to find. The dieter may lose a few pounds only to see the weight return weeks later. A salesperson may read a new book and her sales may take an upward bounce, but usually her performance quickly falls back to prior levels.

Why this consistent lack of success? Our research indicates that much of what has been written and taught about sales excellence has little to do with what really matters. All too many managers, authors, and wizards are dead wrong about what it takes to be a great sales performer.

Put bluntly, we see a number of myths about sales performance pop up again and again. Unfortunately, these misconceptions have guided the sales management practices of too many companies, inadvertently hindering the productivity of their own salespeople. Throughout the pages of this book we will identify these myths and explain how they can impede your performance. We will also show you the compelling picture of sales success that emerges from more than a quarter of a million interviews and decades of research.

One of these myths is that anyone can sell as long as he has enough desire and training. Recently we worked with the manager of a regional mortgage brokerage company. Frank had been in sales management for many years and believed that as long as someone could walk and talk and had enough desire, he could teach that person to sell. As you might guess, quite a few applicants who came through his door met these criteria. So he hired them. And he trained them. And more than 85 percent failed in the first year. Frank's explanation for those who failed was that they just did not have enough desire to succeed.

We came to a different conclusion. *The idea that anyone can sell is nonsense.* Sales simply is not for everyone because consistent success in a sales career requires the presence of certain talents. In the course of our work we have studied sales forces for some of the best companies, companies that have carefully recruited and selected their representatives. Even in the best companies, we found that 35 percent of the sales force did not have the talents necessary to achieve acceptable results predictably. This rather considerable group—one of every three salespeople out there—is consistently in the bottom half of the performance curve.

Compounding this problem is the tendency among many companies to develop and enforce policies designed for these poor producers rather than establish cultures and practices that support great performers. These policies do little to help poor performers get better and sometimes even drive away the best producers. Having put the wrong people in the wrong jobs, many companies waste enormous resources trying to postpone their inevitable failure.

In Frank's case the numbers were even worse than our average. Over two-thirds of the people he hired lacked the talents we see in top performers. He spent much of his time and resources trying to prop up poor performers. Yet to this day, Frank still believes that anyone can sell, and this tenet keeps him from recognizing the rarity of the abilities that his best salespeople possess. Because he fails to recognize the special nature of his top performers, he approaches salary negotiations, territory assignments, and even his own supervisory techniques and practices in a less than optimal fashion. Myths have a way of enduring that defies reason and data.

In our research we have not found any magic sales dust to sprinkle on poor performers to turn them around. Poor performers seem to be immune to both carrots and sticks. On the other hand, this book can show those who *do* have the potential to be great sales performers how to identify and unleash their potential. The recommendations you'll find in *Discover Your Sales Strengths* are about turning good sales performers into great ones, and helping great performers understand how to stay on top.

Why do we focus on great performers? Isn't it good enough just to be good? Not anymore, and not as we look into the future. Maintaining a successful career over forty years is no easy task.

Even great performers may let their performance slip over time. The results can be an unpleasant midlife employment crisis and a scramble in the last twenty years of a career. Look around your own company. How many senior representatives do you find leaving for a comfortable retirement after a sustained successful career? They are few and far between in most companies. It makes you wonder if this performance slide is inevitable. Do we just get tired of doing the same thing year after year?

Evelyn is a sixty-four-year-old pharmaceutical sales representative. She has been in the same territory for the past twenty-five years. Her biggest fear is not old age, but retirement. This is not because of any financial concerns since she has more than enough money to live out her days in a comfortable style. She can't stand the thought of retiring because she loves what she does every day. "I will miss this job so much," she told us. Our research has helped us understand why some people never seem to burn out, continuing year after year with renewed enthusiasm and exceptional results.

Even in the short term we found a big difference between the results of great sales performers and the results of those who are merely good. For example, in a study Gallup completed with a group of sales agents, the average agents sold $2 million to $4 million in new business annually, but the exceptional agents sold in excess of $40 million. Great performance isn't merely twice as good as good; it's exponentially better.

These differences go far beyond higher sales and even higher profitability. They also include greater job satisfaction and a true sense of *engagement* in work. In fact, it's this engagement that produces these exceptional results and directly contributes to building and retaining a core of loyal customers. Our research indicates that the happier you feel about your performance and the greater your satisfaction in your sales role, the more your customers want to buy from you. Salespeople who are merely good may generate acceptable results, but they are less likely to create customer loyalty, and they hardly ever feel the same way about their jobs as Evelyn does.

This book is about becoming engaged in your work. How can you accomplish this? We have found three key points: (1) discover your strengths, (2) find the right fit, and (3) work for the right manager. Let's briefly intro-duce these concepts.

Discover Your Strengths

The power of knowing your strengths is obvious to some, but the majority of us fail to give this important matter any real thought. In fact, a majority of the peo-ple we talked to had limited knowledge of their talents, their innate potential for strength. Trying to build a suc-cessful career without this powerful, important infor-mation is like trying to drive down a highway with a foggy windshield. If we're lucky, we will avoid a head-on collision, but we will most likely miss the important signs that tell us when we need to stop, turn, or yield. Why is it so hard to see our strengths clearly?

Strengths, those capabilities that enable us to perform well in various parts of our lives, spring from recurring patterns of thought, feeling, and behavior that occur spontaneously and become unique parts of our personal-ity as we mature into adults. Since these patterns are such an intrinsic part of us, as natural as breathing, we can take them for granted. People who meet others easily see nothing special about this gift. Empathetic people just as-sume that everyone reacts to the emotions of others as in-stinctively as they do. As a result of the spontaneity with which we apply our talents to various situations, we overlook them and how important and valuable they are.

Our human penchant for fooling ourselves can also cause us to have less than accurate assessments of our abilities. In our "plus columns" we often will list strengths we would like to have instead of those we re-ally possess. We might think we're good with people be-cause we'd like to be. Similarly, we might attribute strengths to ourselves because we believe those in our types of jobs or circumstances are supposed to have those strengths. If we think that successful salespeople are aggressive, or competitive, or disciplined, we might conclude that we must have those strengths because we are successful in sales.

A third reason we can be confused about our strengths is our use of vague language to describe them. One sales representative we interviewed told us that his greatest strength was his "nose for business." He insisted he could smell a good deal a mile away, that he could smell when it was time to go for the close, that he could smell the fear in a competitor. After a while we felt as if we were talking to Lassie. A nose for business may be a colorful metaphor, but it is not very helpful in understanding how to grow and develop. Realistically, we can't develop our strengths until we know what they are and can define them in practical terms.

A fourth reason our strengths are obscured is that most of us have been encouraged to focus on our weaknesses instead of building on our talents to create strengths. Every time we ask about strengths versus weaknesses, we find that more people believe that growth comes from correcting what's wrong rather than building on what's right. The key to substantially improving sales performance, according to this line of reasoning, is to identify and correct weaknesses. Many companies perpetuate this reasoning and focus performance reviews on "areas for improvement," which is often simply a euphemism for "what's wrong with you." How many of us have walked away from an annual review with a list of areas in which we should improve instead of understanding how we can do more of what we do best? Focusing energy on weaknesses might improve performance somewhat, but—contrary to conventional wisdom—great performance comes from strengths. Knowing your talents, understanding them thoroughly, building them into strengths, and seeing how you can put your strengths to work every day is a key to greatness and, our research would attest, the surer path to success.

Our analysis of sales, management, and customer databases showed that the traditional thinking about development was counterproductive. Sales strengths did not spring from education, training, or experience. In almost every company we studied, the best performers and the worst performers were similar in these respects. What set the best performers above the rest was their use of *recurring patterns* to:

- build relationships,
- have an impact on others (and get them to say yes),
- discover and solve customer needs,
- drive their individual performance by focusing on meaningful goals and rewards, and
- find the right structure in which to perform at their best.

Understanding *your* talents in these areas will enable you to build strengths that you can put to work for you every day.

In a later chapter we will discuss strengths in more detail. We will explain fully how your talents become an integral part of your makeup. We will also talk about how you can use your life experiences to help recognize your talents. And we will give you a vocabulary that will help you build and define your strengths.

Also, purchasing this book entitles you to take Gallup's StrengthsFinder, a Web-based interview that will help you identify your talents. After all, no one really knows more about you than you. StrengthsFinder is a highly developed methodology that will help you pick out the most relevant talents you have, talents you can put to use every day.

Find the Right Fit

Understanding your strengths is only the first step in enhancing your performance and job satisfaction. The second step is finding a role that matches your strengths as perfectly as possible.

World-class athletes attain their incredible levels of success because they have found exactly the right sport to play—one in which they can excel constantly. Think about Michael Jordan's success as a basketball player versus his success (or lack thereof) as a baseball player and you'll understand the importance of fit. No one can dispute Jordan's athletic talent. In fact, sportswriters voted him the best athlete of the century. But even someone as gifted as Jordan has to be in the right role for his talent to shine.

In our study of more than 150 sales organizations, we have found that sales positions are as different from one another as one sport is from another. The strengths that make someone an excellent pharmaceutical salesperson are different from those required to excel in selling real estate, or jet engines, or strategic consulting. We have seen firsthand many people with exceptional sales talent—but who are in jobs for which they are ill suited, and so they fail to attain exceptional results. In such situations, hard work and perseverance often lead to ever-increasing levels of frustration and disappointment instead of success.

While the concept of fit seems so obvious, in practice we find it is misunderstood and misapplied by companies and individuals alike.

Peter graduated from one of the leading engineering schools in the country. After graduation he easily found a job working in his field. After a few years he realized that he didn't like engineering work nearly as much as he thought he might when he enrolled in engineering school. When we spoke to him, he remembered that even in college he succeeded more because of his discipline than because of any real love for his classwork. This same discipline helped him become a competent engineer, but Peter was deriving little satisfaction from his work.

Like many of us, Peter went to work every day doing something he was good at but not something he was great at. When the industry Peter worked for encountered some difficult times, his company had to cut its workforce by nearly 50 percent. Peter was let go. Suddenly, work in his field was extremely scarce.

Almost out of desperation, Peter began thinking about how else he might earn a living. When a good friend suggested sales, Peter decided to try it. With his engineering degree and several years of work experience on his résumé, he was able to find a job selling technical products with a company that had an engineering sales force. The sales manager who hired Peter believed he had the potential to become a good salesperson.

After two years the sales manager was sure he had made a mistake. Peter's performance was below average, and the likelihood for improvement seemed remote.

When we interviewed Peter, we found that he did have exceptional sales potential. However, his talents looked quite different from those of high-producing reps who worked for his company. His talent profile was more similar to those of salespeople who excelled as stockbrokers than to those who sold technical products. Armed with this information, Peter took a job with a different company selling financial services products. Today he is one of this company's best producers. Peter finally found a role that was a good match for his strengths.

One of the most common mistakes individuals and

companies make about fit is believing that a person's background, education, or experience is what determines a good fit. Consequently, nurses who want to go into sales may seek jobs in the pharmaceutical or medical device industry. Accountants may try to sell financial products. But fit is not about what we know. Fit is about what we are. Fit is about our talents, not our knowledge. We can acquire new information much more easily than we can acquire new talents. In the chapter that deals with fit we will outline exactly the kinds of questions you should ask to determine if you are in the right selling role. These questions can be valuable tools in helping you decide if a new job is really a better job for you.

Over time companies and industries change. When this happens, it's not unusual for the role of the sales force to change as well. You may have been a perfect fit for your company or industry ten years ago, but now different strengths are required. You may find it more difficult to achieve exceptional results. Even if you are an outstanding salesperson, small changes in fit over time can have a dramatic effect on your performance and job satisfaction. If you are feeling "burned out," this may be what has happened to you.

Sometimes changes in your company can occur almost overnight. A merger or an acquisition, a new and different product line, or a landmark event (such as a shift in government reimbursement or regulation) can trigger marked differences in sales missions. If that happens to you, your best bet may be to find another company. That's how important the right fit is.

A representative at a hospital equipment company, Mark shared the competitiveness and independent nature of many of his peers in the sales force. When the company moved to more of a team-selling approach and compensation policy, Mark and his friends at the company were enraged. How could they have as much as 30 percent of their bonuses hinge on the performance of others? The idea seemed preposterous, but the company felt that market conditions gave it no choice but to move forward with this policy. The result: Mark, along with about 25 percent of the sales force, left to sell for a start-up company that sold to individual physicians and medical groups. There an individual rep could still hold sway.

Of course, not everyone has the opportunity or luxury of finding exactly the right job. If that describes the situation you're in, then you have a different challenge concerning fit. Your challenge is to discover how you can put your talents to best use in your current job. You can reap substantial improvements in your current job by adopting a strengths-based development strategy.

Chances are, you may not be getting the encouragement you need from your company to develop a unique selling approach based on your strengths. This is because many companies wrongly believe that a certain kind of selling "style" is essential for success in their industry. However, when we looked at top performers within any single company, we found a variety of selling approaches and styles. In fact, the best sales performers often had little in common with one another. Instead, they had developed styles that suited them well. *The best salespeople adapt the job to suit their strengths; they do not attempt to change their strengths to fit the job.* (It is much easier to tailor a suit to fit your body than to tailor your body to fit a suit.)

Work for the Right Manager

Finally, our research shows a significant link between great sales performers and their managers. As salespeople, we sometimes take so much of the burden of success on our own shoulders that we underestimate the importance of having the right manager. But when Gallup finds great sales performers, great managers are usually close at hand encouraging and motivating their employees. The best players actually need—and deserve—the most gifted coaches. Salespeople fortunate enough to have the right manager can improve their performance by 20 percent. In many respects, finding the right manager is just as important as finding the right company.

As you read on, we will show you how to get the most from your manager. But beware—mediocre managers can actually stifle your performance, slow your progress, and demotivate you from achieving your best. Worse still, they'll blame you! Bad managers never realize that they, not you, are causing your poor results and impeding your progress. As a salesperson, you are at your best when you are working from your strengths. A manager will be most effective when he or she is building on those strengths to improve your performance. So, a key to your success will be helping your current manager become more effective in supporting you—or finding a new manager who can help you be your best. However, if you use this information only to find fault with your company or your manager, you have missed the point. We want you to understand how to work with your manager and your company to maximize your engagement.

Focusing on You

We are pleased about making Gallup's research more public, especially after decades of gathering data. Until now, most of our sales force research has been available only to a very select group of Gallup clients. Over the years we have assisted these clients in identifying and hiring outstanding sales talent. We have helped many organizations create the right environment and management relationships to enable that talent to flourish. As a result, many of these companies have developed world-class selling organizations.

Now we are making the conclusions of our research available directly to salespeople. Everything we have learned about world-class sales forces is as valuable to individual salespeople as it is to the companies that employ them. However, unlike other selling volumes, this is not a book about sales technique. Nor is it a book filled with inspirational stories to pump you up before you face the world each day. It is, though, a book that can significantly improve your performance, your job satisfaction, and your chances of making the right job changes and career moves. You probably already realize that building a successful career is more than just closing an additional sale this quarter or having a banner year. More than anything, this book is dedicated to helping you achieve a truly rewarding and satisfying career. But reaching this goal has never been more challenging.

The business climate has been changing dramatically over the last forty years, and even more so in the last ten years. Less than a decade ago authors James C. Collins and Jerry I. Porras published their best-selling work *Built to Last*. In their book the authors identified eighteen corporations they characterized among the best in the world and referred to them as visionary companies. Yet before even ten years passed, more than 50 percent of these companies faced considerable difficulties. Some of these great giants have become unprofitable, and many have had to make substantial reductions in their workforces. Seemingly unshakable enterprises such as Boeing, Ford, Hewlett-Packard, Motorola, IBM, and Sony have had serious reversals.

These great companies may well recover, but no matter how good the company you work for is, you cannot put your future entirely in its hands. Even great companies stumble and have setbacks. The days when a salesperson could expect to work for the same company throughout his career are gone forever. Whole industries, which employed legions of salespeople forty years ago, have either disappeared or completely changed the way they sell their products.

As we look into the future, we expect this trend to continue. It's unthinkable that we will be purchasing insurance, automobiles, business products, pharmaceuticals, or anything for that matter, in the same way that we purchased them in the last ten years. Over 97 percent of the senior executives we queried told us they expected their business to get tougher in the next decade. The Internet, globalization, government regulation, telecommunications, and demographics are driving predictable and sometimes not so predictable changes in the way we do business. Sales forces will undergo incredible changes. You can no longer count on your company (or even your industry) to employ salespeople—or the same types of salespeople—indefinitely. The essence of many sales missions will change dramatically. But at the same time, new opportunities will emerge. Because of these trends, you must take charge of your own career and future. We believe our research can help you meet these challenges, and succeed.

You are the CEO of your own career, and planning your future is critical. No visionary company would base its future on half-truths, myths, or misinformation, and neither should you. As you think about your own future, Gallup's databased research can guide you and help you make the most of your potential and your future.

Moving Forward

We make no claim to be wizards ourselves. (We don't look good enough in purple robes and hats to pull off the wizard thing.) We are more like investigative reporters who have examined Gallup's data—data that point to clear, albeit sometimes surprising, conclusions. If anything, research has made us distrustful of wizards and opinions, theories and conjectures, perhaps because so many of our own opinions about great salespeople fell by the wayside as the research piled up.

As it turns out, the wizard we met in New Orleans made an important point—and we consider our six dollars well spent. Perhaps you are wondering what was printed on the cards he handed us. They simply said, "If you have followed the wizard's instructions carefully, then your wish has already begun to come true."

The wizard's last instruction to us was to think about how to get started. If you want to become one of the world's best salespeople, we suggest that a good way to start is to turn the page to the next chapter. There we will comment on many of the myths and misconceptions that have become "conventional wisdom" about sales performance—myths that may be holding you back from greater success. More important, we will share insights from decades of intense research, insights that will result in sustained, improved performance. And, for no extra charge, we will even tell you exactly where you got your shoes.

CHAPTER 2

The Great Sales Myths

It ain't what you don't know that gets you into trouble.
It's what you know for sure that just ain't so.

—MARK TWAIN

Doctors tell us that kidney stones are one of the most painful medical conditions human beings can suffer. These minuscule calcium fragments form in the kidney and eventually get stuck in the ureter, a tiny tube connecting the kidney to the bladder. This causes blockage, infection, and incredible pain.

Fortunately, there's a treatment. Patients sit in a huge water bath while ultrasonic shock waves disintegrate the stones. If all goes well (and it usually does), everything returns to normal. Even so, no one wants to have another kidney stone.

However, people who have had one stone are very likely to have another. So for years physicians placed such patients on low-calcium diets in the hopes of preventing recurrences. This therapy seems to make sense. After all, kidney stones are made up of calcium, so why not cut down on calcium intake? The problem: Patients kept getting more stones. When medical researchers studied the problem, they found that patients with low-calcium diets had 47 percent more stones than patients with normal calcium intake. Doctors had been doing exactly the wrong thing for decades. Ouch!

Data Counts

This example illustrates—rather painfully—the problem with assuming that if something makes sense intuitively, it must be true. Even the assumptions of experts, bosses, and, yes, wizards can collapse under the weight of research. That's why we collected data about sales representatives.

At Gallup, we have always had a penchant for collecting and analyzing data and a healthy suspicion about assumptions and conventional wisdom. Over the past decades we have learned that good research needs to be free from any bias about outcomes or findings. We research to *learn,* rather than to support what we think. So, when we began our research on salespeople, The Gallup Organization had no theories or preconceptions.

We are still learning. For the past forty years we have gathered data specifically about sales and sales performance. While we have gotten very purposeful, particularly over the past couple of decades, we must confess that we began this journey somewhat by accident.

In the mid-1950s Don Clifton, a Ph.D. researcher at the University of Nebraska, was developing a reputation for tackling unusual problems scientifically. One day the head of the Reserve Officers Training Corps (ROTC) came to Don in a quandary. Many students at Nebraska were enrolling in the ROTC program in their freshman year, but only a very small percentage of students stuck with the ROTC through their four years of college and then joined the army. In fact, for every ten students who initially enrolled, only two completed the program. Don was asked to do some research to help them understand why so many recruits were dropping out.

In his characteristic fashion, Don turned the problem around. Realizing that many reasons were behind the program's high dropout rate, he decided it could be more productive instead to ask why people stayed with it. Did the recruits who stuck with the program share some characteristics, and could he harness his knowledge about those characteristics to select other recruits who were likely to stay?

Don's research background had taught him that if you want to understand something . . . ask. So, during extensive interviews he asked hundreds of different questions. He was looking for questions that were answered in a similar fashion by those recruits who stayed, but differently by those who quit. Eventually he had a list of questions that met his criteria.

Armed with these questions, he interviewed all prospective recruits in the coming year and used his analysis of their answers to make predictions about their program longevity. Sure enough, his predictions turned out to be largely correct. As a result, the ROTC used Don's instrument to select new recruits.

Within a few short years the retention numbers reversed: Eight out of ten recruits were completing the program. News of this impressive turnaround spread quickly. The chancellor at the University, Clifford Hardin, who had an association with a large life insurance company, took an interest in these unusual results because the insurance industry was plagued with high turnover. Many people were hired right out of college to be insurance sales agents, but very few were successful.

Hardin asked Clifton if his methods might be used to select life insurance sales agents who would have a greater
likelihood of success.

Don was eager to do additional research. For some
time he had had an interest in investigating the reasons
such variations exist among individuals in job performance. Looking for the best way to study the differences
among human beings that might account for achievement, Don was stymied at first by the lack of objective
criteria for so many positions. Who were the best teachers, or counselors, or leaders? Don found so much dis-
agreement on assessment of performance in these roles.
However, life insurance companies maintained detailed
records of every sales agent's performance. For Don this
was an excellent population to study to extend his research.

Essentially, he used the same process he had used
with the ROTC recruits. He tested hundreds of questions looking for those that were answered similarly by
the most productive sales representatives, but differently by the rest of the sales force. When he was sure
that he had a satisfactory list of questions, he began interviewing new sales recruits whom the life insurance
company planned to hire. Based on how well a recruit's
answers matched a statistical model of the best producers, Don made a prediction about how well each candidate would do as a life insurance salesperson. Sure
enough, those candidates who Don identified outsold
the rest of the recruits significantly.

On the strength of these results, we began to help
companies evaluate sales candidates. As we conducted
in-depth interviews for these companies, we came into
direct contact with thousands and thousands of salespeople.

Early Discoveries

To date, Gallup has interviewed hundreds of thousands of sales representatives. To our knowledge, this is the largest database of information about sales professionals in the world. In most instances we began our work with clients by conducting detailed face-to-face or phone interviews with their sales representatives. We were then supplied information about the productivity of each representative and were able to compare how they responded on our interview to their productivity figures. When we examined productivity, we usually found a range of performance like that depicted in the following graph.

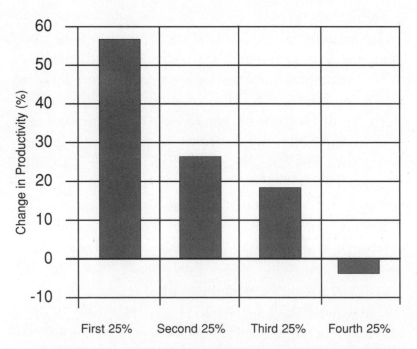

In this graph you can see that the top 25 percent of the sales force is producing 57 percent of the business increases. The bottom 25 percent is actually in negative territory.

Although the actual numbers varied from company to company, we always found a significant range in performance when we compared the top quartile to the bottom quartile. When we looked at the very best performers—those individuals consistently in the top 10 percent—it was not unusual to find sales reps producing ten times more than the average performers in the same sales force. Our goal was to identify the characteristics and talents of a company's very best salespeople to help those companies hire only people with the potential to become stars.

The companies we worked with tended to have well-established sales forces and well-established hiring guidelines. These guidelines, whether formal or informal, represented senior managers' views about what it took to be successful in their particular industries. As we began to compare our data against companies' guidelines, we began to appreciate just how many misconceptions existed about great sales performers, even among seasoned sales managers.

Bear in mind, we started our research in the early 1960s, and some of the attitudes we heard from sales managers seem almost unbelievable today. For example, we frequently heard that women did not belong in sales. Equipment manufacturers told us that their products were far too heavy for women to lug around. Medical device manufacturers told us that operating room supervisors preferred to have attractive young men call on them. Financial services companies told us that women would have no credibility selling stocks and bonds.

Of course, such opinions are laughable, but even then we found that the characteristics that marked great sales performers were present in both men and women. The talents that make great sales professionals are not gender, race, or age specific. Yet many notions and hiring guidelines back then were. Admittedly, our goal was not to make a case for diversity, but when companies started to focus on talent, diversity happened.

Some companies developed their own unique prejudices or misconceptions about sales excellence. One client liked to hire only attractive people. This company's national sales meeting looked like a Ken and Barbie convention. Does appearance play a role in sales success? We can find no evidence to support the notion that the best-looking people sell the most. The sales profession is not a beauty pageant.

We found some companies that preferred hiring people who had played team sports in high school or college. A sports background, some companies reasoned, must mean that these recruits would be more competitive than others and would make good team players. Other companies wanted to hire people only from certain schools, or people who had been in the military. Still others hired only people who were from the same geography as their territory. If you were from New York, you could not sell in the South, they reasoned, and vice versa. Of course, none of these preferences had anything to do with sales performance. As our studies soon demonstrated, there is no correlation between results and such factors. We can't claim that we were very surprised that these notions were quickly proven false. But some of our findings did surprise us.

The Big Lie

Take a look at the following ad. You have probably seen hundreds of similar ads in newspapers. Can you spot the line that contains a myth about sales performance?

WANTED
Personable Sales Professional
3–5 years experience
College degree (MBA preferred)
Unlimited income for those with the drive to succeed!
Just follow our step-by-step proven method

If you guessed every line, you're on the right track. We found so many misconceptions about sales performance that we began to think of them collectively as the "big lie." What are these misconceptions? We'll call them myths, and they are as follows: the education myth, the experience myth, the a-good-salesperson-can-sell-anything myth, the right sales approach myth, the training myth, the relationship myth, the money myth, and the desire myth.

All of them appear in this ad. (Okay, we wrote this ad ourselves, but we bet you have seen plenty of similar ads.)

These myths still influence many companies' hiring decisions. They also influence policies affecting the management of their salespeople. In fact, they have hindered the development of many salespeople and stopped them from reaching their full potential. Let's look at some of these myths in more detail.

THE EDUCATION MYTH

Do you know what Bill Gates, Harry Truman, and Dave Thomas all have in common? Bill Gates is, of course, the founder of Microsoft and as of this writing the wealthiest man on the planet. Harry Truman was the thirty-third president of the United States, capping a career that included a successful business venture and a stint as a county judge. Dave Thomas was the founder of the Wendy's hamburger chain. Dave was also one of the driving forces behind the success of the Kentucky Fried Chicken restaurants.

Given these substantial accomplishments, you might be surprised to learn that none of these individuals completed college. In fact, Dave Thomas dropped out of high school. In his later years he did get his GED equivalency, quipping that if he had only graduated from high school sooner, he might have been able to open up more restaurants.

Bill Gates, Harry Truman, and Dave Thomas are not the only non–college grads to make good. *Forbes* magazine's list of the wealthiest four hundred individuals for the year 2001 included 118 people who never completed college. Incidentally, 118 represents about half of those on the list who did not inherit their money. Even without college educations, these individuals managed to amass an average wealth of $1.8 billion. If only they had studied harder and gotten better grades.

We live in a society that values education. Think back to the questions you were asked on every job interview: What was your grade point average? What college did you attend? Do you have an advanced degree? Some companies even want to know your SAT scores. Such questions have become increasingly common in a competitive business climate.

Many professions have stringent educational prerequisites. You have every reason to expect your doctor to have a medical degree and your accountant to have been schooled in tax laws and regulations. Engineering, law, and teaching are all professions requiring specific educational backgrounds. The trend toward higher education has appeared in the selling profession as well.

Naturally, we were curious about the relationship between education and sales performance. Even though more and more companies are demanding certain education levels of their hires, does that education have any bearing on success?

Some time ago one of our financial services clients informed us that it had decided to hire only MBAs from the best business schools as sales representatives. It believed its products and its customers were becoming more sophisticated, and it wanted a sales force that could keep pace with the rapid changes in the marketplace. This company believed that if a little education was good, more would be even better.

We did a quick study of its existing sales force and found that one-third of those already employed had MBAs. If education consistently made a difference in outcomes, we should have found that the best performers were more educated than the average performers. We should have found a concentration of MBAs among the top performers. We assembled a performance graph similar to the one illustrated a few pages earlier and broke the sales force down into four performance quartiles. *We found that most of the individuals in the top quartile did not have advanced degrees. In fact, most of the best performers had not achieved high grade point averages in college.*

When we pointed this out to the company managers, they shrugged their shoulders and insisted that the future would require a better-educated sales force. So they proceeded with this policy change and began to require that all sales representatives take night courses to get advanced degrees. Why? Because this company believed the education myth—that schooling would miraculously transform its sales force.

This company found out pretty quickly that education wasn't the key to the transformation it wanted. Many superior performers threatened to leave rather than attend night school. And what became of the new crop of MBAs? Three months into their tenure with the company, one-third of them had not yet realized that they had been hired to sell. They were waiting in their offices for clients to call them. These MBAs might have learned the history of sales. They might have learned the importance of sales. They might have taken courses on how to sell. They might have even been asked to teach a course on sales. But knowledge and action are two vastly different things. As it turned out, the acquisition of an MBA had little to do with the ability to sell stocks and bonds.

But what about companies with especially technical products? Another client we work with sells highly sophisticated computer equipment. In an effort to improve its sales force, it decided to hire only electrical engineers with at least a 3.5 grade point average. Once again, when we looked at those individuals consistently in the top of the company's sales force, we found that very few met the new standard the company wanted to impose on its new hires. Inadvertently the new standard would have disqualified many of the company's top performers. Ironically, the company's very best sales performer was a college dropout. Before going into sales, he had worked as a roadie for a well-known rock band.

This former roadie did not have the educational credentials the company wanted, and yet he was its best performer. He did have the aptitude that enabled him to learn about the product and its application. Most important, he understood that customers were more interested in what the products could do than in how they worked. (We asked him how his equipment worked and he told us, "It works fine!") His strengths enabled him to surpass many better-educated rivals who communicated so much technical information that they confused customers and frequently lost sales.

Why would a company set up hiring criteria that

could potentially screen out many of its top performers? Because it believes the education myth.

Are these companies' sales forces the exceptions to the rule? We don't believe so. We can tell you that in all the companies we have studied we have *never*—even in very technical fields—found a relationship between education and sales success.

We mention the education myth because over the course of your career you are likely to have a number of different sales jobs. The average longevity in a sales position is less than five years. That means that in an average forty-year career, you are likely to have as many as eight different jobs!

Each time you're looking for a new position, you have a chance to find a sales role that is a more perfect match with your strengths. But education is frequently not a good indicator of talents. Don't limit the choice of your sales options only to careers that mirror your educational background.

Some companies have educational blinders when it comes to recruiting salespeople. However, more companies are beginning to realize how diverse their top performers are and how unproductive it can be to set up the wrong screening requirements.

THE EXPERIENCE MYTH

In some professions experience matters a great deal and has a huge relationship with success. If you need open-heart surgery, you should go to the cardiac surgeon who has performed the most procedures since studies show that complication rates for surgical procedures go down directly in relationship to the experience of the surgeon. We have found that sales, however, is not an experience-sensitive profession in the same way that surgery is.

The learning curve in most sales jobs is usually short. Discounting data from very recent recruits, *we only rarely find a strong correlation between experience and results.* Salespeople with ten years of experience in the same companies or industries do not necessarily sell more than those with five years under their belts. Individuals with five years' experience do not necessarily sell more than people with three years' experience.

However, many companies place great weight on experience, and herein lies the trap. If you are performing at only an average level, it could well be because your strengths are not the right "fit" for what you do every day. You might be thinking about a change. But when the headhunters call, the job they want to talk to you about is probably similar to the job you already have. Companies want to hire you for your experience. You might even feel more comfortable taking a job that matches your experience.

If you are not careful when changing jobs, however, you will only be changing one poorly fitting job for another—even if the new company is better positioned in the market, or its products are better. However, if you are already a great performer, such a move could be a big career enhancement because the fit is already right.

The problem with sales experience is that it can delude you about your capabilities. You will probably get "up to speed" more quickly and need less training in a job that is similar to your former job. However, if you are average, all you will do is get back up to average more quickly than you did before. "More of the same" from an average performer is not likely to move you from average to great, but improving the "fit" will.

THE A-GOOD-SALESPERSON-CAN-SELL-ANYTHING MYTH

From time to time we have run into salespeople who have done a good job in several different sales capacities. However, such all-around naturals are rare. Instead, we have found repeatedly that salespeople who do the best in any company share a configuration of strengths that are well matched to their roles. Thus, salespeople might do an exceptional job in one situation and a mediocre job in another. No number of pep talks will correct this situation. They might also feel disgruntled, not realizing that their discontent stems from not using their strengths.

Sometimes it takes a few career changes to find exactly the right sales role. Glena is the top residential home salesperson in her area. Year after year she sells more homes than anyone else and is constantly breaking her own records. When she talks about her work, it is easy to see how engaged she is. When her previous clients prepare to sell their homes, Glena is the person they call. But success was not always so easy.

She began her career selling commercial real estate, viewing it as the most prestigious and respected business within the company. It was also a more difficult job to get. Glena's agency would hire anyone to sell residential real estate, but they were very picky about the people they put on the commercial side of the business.

Much to her disappointment, though, Glena never did as well as she hoped to in commercial real estate. "In my very first year I made it to the middle of the pack," she told us. "And that's where I stayed." Her manager was satisfied. She was selling her share, and she was easy to work with. But just being average frustrated Glena. No matter what she did, she never really improved her standing. "I was so discouraged. Sometimes I thought I should give up sales altogether."

But she didn't. Instead, she moved over to residential sales. Much to her surprise, she loved it. Glena had not been able to use her strengths fully selling commercial real estate, but in her new role she was able to use her imagination to show prospective homeowners the potential of particular houses. She also has a personality that makes her a pleasant companion, someone with whom out-of-town home prospects could feel comfortable spending several days at a time. This trait has helped her capture a good portion of the transferees moving into her neighborhood from out-of-town areas. While the difference between commercial real estate sales and residential sales might seem subtle, our experience suggests that even subtle changes can make big differences in a person's success.

Very often today we find that companies change their sales missions or their ways of going to market without realizing that their existing sales forces are not the right fit for the new venture. Cross-selling or synergistic product offerings have become popular growth strategies. Companies wrongly assume that because they have good sales forces they can layer any new product or service onto them. But even slight changes can have big impacts.

One of our clients has a large sales force that sells property and casualty insurance. Without question some of their salespeople are the best in the industry. So, the company decided to use this sales force to sell life insurance. If they'd had to compete against other property and casualty agents to sell these products, they might have been successful. But their competition was highly talented life insurance salespeople. Even the company's best representatives struggled.

Similarly, the sales force at a medical supplies company called on nurses as their primary customers for years. Suddenly, a new product was introduced that required salespeople to call on physicians. The sales force did not adapt well to this change at all. Slight product changes can often require a very different kind of salesperson, and companies—or salespeople—will have to make the necessary adjustments.

Finding the right role is one of the most important career challenges you'll face. One of the key purposes of this book is to help you uncover information about yourself that can be really valuable in helping you find that "just right" role.

THE RIGHT SALES APPROACH MYTH

We are constantly surprised at the dissimilarities of the sales approaches of the best people we have studied. Within the same industry, and even within the same company, we find very different and yet equally successful approaches to the sales process.

Yet companies often assume that a certain style of selling is more conducive to their industry than other styles. A company might decide that all their people should be "consultants," and so they will endeavor to retrain the entire sales force on a new selling method. But is there one right sales approach?

One salesperson we have followed is consistently in the top 10 percent of his sales force. His sales manager recounted to us the first time he worked with this particular representative in the field. "Tom had a reputation for producing outstanding results year after year, so I was really looking forward to working with him. When we made our first sales call, I thought I was being set up for some kind of practical joke. I had never heard anyone give such a clumsy presentation. It was so bad, I was tempted to grab the product out of Tom's hand and continue the presentation myself. Much to my surprise, as Tom concluded his rambling explanation, the customer just nodded her head and agreed to bring in a trial order.

"On the second sales call I saw more of the same. Over the next few days I realized this was no practical joke. Tom really did give poorly flowing presentations. Still, his customers did not seem to mind this at all. Why? Because he has been able to develop an important relationship with his customers—a relationship based on trust. He was always very careful in looking at a new account to make sure he started with a product that would be exactly right for the customer. Once Tom makes an initial sale, he is frequently able to expand the business because his customers have begun to trust him. Not because he gives stellar presentations."

In the same sales force, another individual is also routinely in the top 10 percent. This person has little in the way of relationship-building strengths, but is incredibly persuasive. His presentations are so compelling that his customers can't help but say yes when he asks for their order.

These highly successful individuals have developed their own unique styles, styles built around their strengths. For one to try to imitate the other would spell disaster. *Rookie sales managers, or even poor veterans, sometimes wrongheadedly believe their job is to get everyone to sell the same way they do.* Fortunately, Tom had a sales manager who understood that while Tom's approach was unconventional, it made good use of Tom's real strengths.

That is not to say that you cannot constantly hone your sales approach. You can, but bear in mind that developing a unique style can take time. Be open-minded about trying new things because it's often difficult to know ahead of time what will work for you. However, if you feel uncomfortable with something new after a while, don't hesitate to drop it. But then, move forward and try something else.

Is there a right sales approach? Yes, but it is one that is built around your strengths, not on the industry or the products or what someone else is doing. The best salespeople often have highly idiosyncratic methods, but they are the right methods for them.

THE TRAINING MYTH

When we asked the best salespeople if they were taught to sell, they invariably answered yes. This would lead us to believe that training is an important ingredient in sales success. However, when we asked people in the bottom ranks if they were taught to sell, they also invariably answered yes.

It's also hard to ignore the fact that while most of a company's representatives will go through exactly the same initial training program, there is a big difference in the results that those sales representatives generate. Why?

Someone can take art lessons and follow up with more art lessons, but the lessons alone will not turn any individual into a Rembrandt.

We don't want to imply that training cannot help. But training helps those with the inherent strengths and fit much more than it helps poor performers. However, much of the training that companies provide is directed toward poor performers.

You are probably the best person to understand whether more training will help you and to decide what that training should entail. Will more information about your products, your competitors, or your industry help you? Attending seminars on sales techniques might help, but you must be selective in choosing techniques that are a good match for your strengths.

THE RELATIONSHIP MYTH

We are almost reluctant to write this because we can already hear the chorus of objections as we comment on the relationship myth.

"Well, maybe relationships don't matter in certain situations," our readers might say, "but in *our* industry, relationships *are* everything." We have yet to find an industry in which this is completely true.

The notion that relationships are critical to selling is so widely held that everyone assumes it must be true. And in part it is. People with strong people skills frequently use those strengths to generate positive results. But we also see people with great relationship abilities who are not able to sell a thing. Why?

Because relationship strengths themselves are not enough. More than seventy-five years ago Dale Carnegie wrote his famous book *How to Win Friends and Influence People*. The second half of his title is worth considerable attention. The best salespeople influence others . . . they don't just make friends. The best salespeople ask customers for commitments in a way that gets positive results. They are not afraid to risk the relationship to ask for the business. Gaining customers requires more than just making friends.

Surprisingly, we have found a good number of top salespeople who have only average people skills, but they do have the ability to influence others. They have adopted a selling style that works for them and have figured out how to make the most of the relationship abilities they possess. Some—in fact, the vast majority—will never be the "life of the party," and they may not have tremendous amounts of charisma. Some of the best salespeople we met actually limit customer contacts and avoid too much socializing with customers. But boy, can they ask for the order.

One time we were riding around with one of the top salespeople at a client company. She had a territory in one of the nation's largest cities, and, as luck would have it, we were conducting this particular job observation in the dead of a hot summer. Visiting one of Anne's largest clients, we were stunned that on the walls and door of his office were taped about three dozen Christmas scenes drawn by children. When the customer had to leave his office for a minute, we turned to Anne to ask why these Christmas scenes were in his office in August. She looked at us quizzically, then said, "Oh my, I never noticed that before." When the director returned, we asked him the same question. He told us that he thought the Christmas season was the best time of the year and kept his children's pictures up all year so that he could be reminded of it.

Anne, who outsold all of her competitors with this gentleman, overlooked some rather obvious information that some other reps would have used to deepen their ties with him.

What is the most natural way for you to develop relationships, and what is the most natural way for you to move others to commitment? Understanding this vital information about yourself will help you develop your true potential.

THE MONEY MYTH

We have met very few salespeople whose ambition is poverty. Okay, we have not met any! We have also met very few salespeople who are solely "coin operated," as one representative put it. True, money is important to everyone at some level, but no one reward is equally important to everyone in any profession. Not all actors are motivated by fame, not all doctors are motivated by patient care, and not all salespeople are motivated by money.

Even salespeople who have a strong desire to earn significant incomes are often motivated by other factors as well. Our research shows that motivation is often very different for different salespeople. What is important is for *you* to understand what drives *you*. To perform at your best, you need to be in a situation in which you are getting the rewards that are important to you. Those rewards can be complex.

Often we find that companies that offer exceptional income potential to their sales representatives might offer little else. Other companies might offer a dash of recognition or an occasional contest. These "crumbs" are often not enough to satisfy many salespeople's inner motivational needs.

If you are unmotivated, you might feel the need to push yourself more and more just to go out and do your job every day. As long as there is a great income opportunity, you might feel that you should be motivated. But it's easy to underestimate how not having *all* your motivational requirements met can significantly lower your performance. *We have met countless successful salespeople who did poorly in school. Why? Because school did not provide the right motivational rewards to satisfy them.* Once they were in an environment that did, they soared. Sometimes without realizing it we move out of the right motivational environment, and our performance suffers.

A friend of ours tells us that when he was a kid his parents always thought he had a poor appetite. "But that was not it at all," he said, "I just didn't like the food they served."

What's the right food for you? Maybe money is your "thing" and maybe it's not. We have found phenomenal sales reps who are happy to earn $80,000 a year, and we have found phenomenal sales reps who are discontented when earning $300,000. If you're like the very best reps we have studied, your motivation is not one-dimensional.

Sales representatives are often motivated by a desire to feel significant, or by competition, or by a desire to be in charge. Some salespeople have an intense need for the respect of their colleagues or customers. Some get a kick out of opening new accounts, whereas others might feel a keen sense of satisfaction from restoring a broken-down territory back to financial health. When these desires are strongly present in a person's psychological makeup, they must be met or that person's motivation will decline sharply.

THE DESIRE MYTH

Motivation is critical to excellent performance, but it alone is not enough. Our society sends the message that people can do anything they want to do as long as they are willing to work hard and make it happen. We hear this from elementary school on, but in the back of our minds, we know this just isn't true.

Many people could never make it through medical school no matter how strongly they want to be doctors. And just because a person wants to be a famous movie actress, a rock-and-roll singer, or a professional athlete, it doesn't mean it's going to happen. No matter how much people want success or are willing to work for it, they still need something more. And we are not talking about lucky breaks.

People need the appropriate strengths in order to be successful in a given occupation. In sales, strengths stemming from motivational themes are indeed important to an individual's success. You might have your own vocabulary for these striving themes; you might think of them as determination, drive, persistence, or "fire in the belly." *But motivation, by itself, is not sufficient if you are to become a superior salesperson.* Whatever your terminology, such strengths are exceedingly important only when they are accompanied by the requisite strengths in the other areas in sales.

In professional sales these other areas of requisite strengths normally include thinking abilities to help you solve customer problems. The ability to form productive relationships and impact others in a positive way are also important areas of talent. And finally, organizational talent to help you plan your work and follow through on customer commitments is required.

Most important, these talents need to be appropriate for the selling role you are in. For example, some sales jobs require that you meet new customers every day. You might have only one shot at a customer. Maybe you are in a business in which it's unlikely you'll ever see that customer again regardless of whether they buy. On the other hand, you may have to sustain a productive business relationship with the same customer over several years. These are very different relationship talents.

So, simply being motivated isn't enough. It is critically important to possess other sales talents and to find the right match.

Take Donna, for example. Donna is well educated and articulate, and she possesses an incredibly strong desire to succeed. After completing her MBA, she was employed by a regional brokerage firm. However, she was unhappy in that situation and felt that the products her company offered really didn't meet her clients' needs. When an opportunity came up for her to join a well-known national brokerage company, she was ecstatic.

At this point, we interviewed Donna. We found that while she had many impressive attributes, she lacked the spontaneous responses that would allow her to push people into making decisions. Based on our research, the most successful people we interviewed at this brokerage firm were quite comfortable with "pushing" customers along when necessary.

We discussed this issue with Donna and her prospective manager. Donna felt that if she were selling a product that she really believed in, she would be more willing to push people along. The sales manager was so taken with her other attributes that he went ahead and offered her the position.

Three months later we had a follow-up conversation with the sales manager, who told us how hard Donna was working and what excellent progress she had made. She had truly thrown herself into the task of understanding all of her company's products. The manager remarked that he had never seen someone get off to such a fast start.

At six months the manager was still glowing in his reports about Donna. She was now getting out in front of customers on a daily basis and starting to make some real progress. His expectations for her future were high.

At nine months Donna walked in and resigned. She told her manager and us that she had started to really hate the job. She didn't like the constant pressure of having to ask people to buy things. She enjoyed explaining the products to her prospects, but when it came to asking them to make a decision, she just could not do it.

For Donna there was a happy outcome. We worked with her to help her understand her real strengths and were happy to see her take a position that capitalized on those strengths. She teamed up with another representative who loves making initial sales calls and starting up new accounts but does not have Donna's talents for follow-up and subsequent account growth. Now Donna's desire to succeed is on fire because she is doing something that she does well *every day*. She is involved with customers in a way that she loves and is making much more money for herself and for her company.

How About You?

As you can see, the "big lie" has many components. Each one is alive and well, and each one can prevent you from reaching your true sales potential.

Yes, your education and your experience can help you get a particular job. Many companies are impressed by these qualifications and use them as key determinants in hiring one person over another. Just because many companies are fooled about their importance, don't you be.

The sales role for which you're best suited might have nothing to do with your educational background or lack thereof. Similarly, don't stay trapped in the same field just because of your experience. Many salespeople end up in a particular sales role by accident. Whether by luck, accident, or good planning we all get our first job in some particular industry. After a few years we might mistakenly believe that our best career option is to continue in an area in which we have gained experience. But experience, like education, can be inadvertently tilting you away from a role for which you are more ideally suited.

Your underlying strengths are much more relevant than your education or your experience. That is why understanding your strengths is so important. Most people we have interviewed have some strengths that allow them to do something better than a hundred other people or in some cases a thousand other people. What is it that you can do better than a thousand other people? Identifying those strengths and being in a situation in which you can use those strengths in your job every day is what results in exceptional performance. Furthermore, understanding your strengths will help you develop a sales approach that is exactly the right approach for you. Understanding your strengths will help you pick out the kind of training that will be most helpful for you and adopt techniques that are in alignment with your talents.

CHAPTER 3

Strengths:
A Capacity for Near-Perfect Performance

The most important understanding you can gain about yourself is your strengths and the underlying talents that make them possible.

Anatomy of a Strength

What makes up a strength? What gives a person a capacity for near-perfect performance on a consistent basis? As you think about that question, you may find yourself disagreeing with some of the comments we made in the previous chapter on myths. You may feel that at least some of your experiences and training have contributed to your performance. In all probability you are correct.

Training and experience can make an enormous difference in our performance. Luciano Pavarotti, the world-famous tenor, sings more beautifully because of the years of voice training he has had. Johnnie Cochran is much better in front of the jury after years of experience than he was on his first day in court. Yet when we try to define our strengths based on our experience, our training, or our education, we miss the most important and essential ingredient of a strength.

Let's illustrate this point with a hypothetical example. Suppose we took ten individuals who had never typed anything before and asked them to sit down and prepare a letter. The outcome would be pretty much as you might expect. These people would type painfully slowly, and their work would be filled with errors.

Now suppose we put each one of these individuals through a three-month training program in which they had the chance to learn and practice typing skills. Then, for the next nine months we had each of them work in a job that required a considerable amount of typing every day. What would be the results at the end of this time period? Would everyone type equally well?

We can tell you from our analysis of many occupations that we would find a considerable range in performance, even when training and experience levels are almost identical, and even in seemingly simple occupations such as typing. One or two of these individuals are likely to have become excellent typists. A few would become passable typists, and still others would find typing to be tedious, and their work would still be filled with mistakes. Yes, all of them would be better than the day they started, but only a small percentage would end up capable of delivering a near-perfect performance consistently.

Since they all had the same training and experience, we know that training and experience are not what drives the difference in performance. This, incidentally, is why we refer to training and experience as myths. What is accountable for the difference? If we looked at the very best typists, we would find that they had a combination of physical dexterity (especially in their fingers), an ability to concentrate on their work, and a temperament that allowed them to do the same kind of work all day long and still perform at an exceptional level.

These are not characteristics that come from training, experience, or knowledge. These characteristics are best described as underlying talents. Our best typing recruits had these talents in abundance before they ever touched a keyboard, while some of our other recruits had almost none. These underlying talents ultimately differentiated how well each of these recruits performed.

Of course, training and experience and knowledge play a role. Even the most talented of our recruits could not type a lick until they acquired some knowledge about how to type. Then they had to have an opportunity to practice and develop their skill. And finally, they had to hone this skill through their day-to-day experience.

Strengths are enhanced by our experiences, our skills, and our knowledge. But the most important underlying component is talent. Without the right talents, all the experience, training, and knowledge will never turn us into world-class performers. We cannot understand or develop our real strengths until we understand our underlying talents.

What Is Talent?

Even though talent is all around us, most of us have a very unclear idea of what talent is and so we fail to see it in ourselves and others. We may mistakenly believe that great talent is something possessed by only a few gifted artists, athletes, or performers.

One reason we fail to recognize talent is that we tend to think of talent on much too broad a level. Take musical talent as an example. A concert pianist, a lyricist, a singer, and an orchestra conductor all have musical talent. But the underlying talents of each of these individuals can be markedly different. A concert pianist needs a tremendous amount of physical control with his hands and an intuitive sense of rhythm and timing just for starters. He also needs to be able to have each hand do something different at the same time. A lyricist, on the other hand, needs to be good with words. Her talents run more toward the poetic. A singer needs great vocal cords and a melodious tone, whereas a conductor needs to keep fifty different musical parts in his head as he tries to create a balanced sound. All of these individuals are musically talented, but they are all different.

Defining sales talent turned out to be just as elusive. We finally came to the conclusion that there is no such thing as sales talent. Or, to phrase it more correctly, there is no such *single* thing as sales talent. We found sales talent to be just as varied as musical talent. Sales talent comes in many different configurations. The underlying talents of great salespeople can be vastly different.

When we looked carefully at the best salespeople, we found that they were remarkably dissimilar. Some were competitive; some were not. Some were great communicators; some were not. Some were very disciplined, and some were among the most disorganized people we have met.

As we began interviewing more and more great salespeople, we found countless varieties of configurations of great performers. This observation held true even when we looked within the same industry or company.

Yet even in Gallup's earliest research we had discovered an important key. We found that the best salespeople in any company answered certain questions differently from their more average-producing counterparts. New sales candidates who also answered those same questions similarly tended to become exceptional salespeople for that company as well. These predictive questions indicated that some common threads existed among the best producers, especially within a given sales role.

Over time we could see a correlation developing in the kinds of questions that were most predictive. They were not questions about a candidate's experience or track record or educational background. Nor were they questions about facts and knowledge pertaining to their industry. *The most predictive questions tended to be about what a person was like as opposed to what that person knew or had done.* The best questions revealed a person's spontaneous responses. These questions exposed patterns about how a candidate thought, felt, and behaved. From this we crafted a definition of talent. It is a pattern of thought, feeling, or behavior that can be productively applied.

In our studies of the talents most indicative of success, we found that they can be grouped into areas we call *themes*. Like a theme that runs through a novel, talent themes, when strongly present, run through a person's life. In many ways these themes define a person. They serve as a language for describing human talents and are thereby extremely useful tools for developing strengths.

Our understanding of talent began to crystallize around specific themes. Empathy is an example of such a theme. Some people are much more attuned to the feelings of others. They seem automatically to be able to put themselves in other people's shoes and understand their feelings. Highly empathetic people are able to pick up on another person's happiness or sadness or worries and they do it almost automatically without conscious effort. Most important, they have a way of conveying their understanding to the other person.

We found that many of the highly successful life insurance salespeople we interviewed were highly empathetic. They were able to use their empathy as a way to build relationships quickly with a prospective customer and establish trust. Since most life insurance sales calls happen in a single evening, this theme of Empathy was highly advantageous. Most of us, as customers, respond more favorably to someone we feel understands us.

We also found that buying life insurance is a decision many people try to postpone. Most young couples with small children have an unending list of items they want and need, all of which seem much more pressing and immediate than a life insurance policy.

Not surprisingly, most prospects at the end of a presentation want to "think it over." Even though they may agree that they should have life insurance, their sales resistance starts to take over and they become reluctant. We found another theme common in the best life insurance salespeople that helped them deal with just such situations. This is a theme we call Command. People with strong Command feel quite comfortable imposing their views on others. They are not put off by confrontation, and the more resistance a prospect shows, the more determined they become to close the sale. People with strong Command have no qualms about getting other people to face up to some of the unpleasant facts we have to deal with in our lives. Command is a theme that can help a salesperson ask for the order and keep asking even in the face of objections and resistance. No wonder we found so many highly successful life insurance salespeople brimming over with Command talents.

So, are we saying that if you have strong Empathy and strong Command you would make an outstanding life insurance salesperson? Possibly, but not necessarily. Selling is a complex activity. Calibrating talents to a particular sales role is more complicated than just the presence or absence of two themes. We will discuss this in more detail in a later chapter that describes "fit." In this chapter we are simply using Empathy and Command as examples.

What we are saying is that the talent themes that are strongly pronounced in us are the keys to building strengths and delivering exceptional performance. The best explanation for why some people were successful in one sales role and others were successful in a different sales role had to do with the unique configuration of themes present in each performer.

How Do These Patterns Develop?

Where do these patterns—these talents—come from? How do they develop? If we don't like the patterns that have become a part of our inherent makeup, can we change them?

Since we're talking about patterns of thought, feeling, and behavior, we can look at the process by which our brains develop for an answer. After all, thoughts, feelings, and behaviors all emanate from the brain. As our brain develops, so do these patterns.

When you were born, you had around one hundred billion brain cells or neurons. This is about the same number you'll have most of your life (give or take the few hundred million you sacrificed when you were partying at school). The brain stores information by making connections among brain cells. Each brain cell is capable of making in the range of fifteen thousand connections. These connections help us process new information as we receive it. They also influence how we respond to situations. If someone waves a greeting at you, you are likely to wave back. You do this spontaneously, without thinking. This response is evidence of your brain cell connections at work.

This process of making connections, or synaptic threads as they are sometimes called, begins even before we are born and continues at a rapid pace until we are about three years old. Then the process of making new connections seems to stop. For the next twelve to fifteen years the brain is actually pruning out those threads that are hardly ever used while it is strengthening others.

Various researchers have described this process by comparing the human brain to a forest. Every bit of information that we receive in the first three years is like an animal walking through the forest, leaving behind a trail or path where it has tracked. After three years there will be hundreds, if not thousands, of these pathways through the forest. (In the brain the number is significantly larger.) During the next several years some of those pathways will be used over and over again, becoming increasingly better defined. Other paths will get almost no use whatsoever, and gradually the forest will grow in and reclaim that land as the path falls into disuse. After twelve to fifteen years some of those paths have completely disappeared. Others have widened into trails, still others have become one-lane roads, others have become main streets, and others have become superhighways.

That means that somewhere between the ages of fifteen and eighteen these patterns are completely formed, and this process stops. The patterns of thought, feeling, and behavior that will last a lifetime have developed. If a person has lots of discipline, empathy, or competitiveness, it's likely to have manifested itself by that point. Some researchers refer to this process as the brain becoming "wired."

These patterns form in response to millions and millions of stimuli, experiences, and information that we have absorbed and cataloged. Since no two persons' stimuli or experiences are the same, everyone is wired somewhat differently. These patterns, which endure for your lifetime, make you a unique individual.

The main point is that our brains eventually become wired, and after that time frame it's increasingly difficult to change this wiring. For example, if you're wired in such a way that you relish the opportunity to meet new people, this is a pattern that will stay with you throughout your adult life. It's a pattern you can depend on. Similarly, if you do not have a pattern of competition, you will not develop one later in life.

Does this mean we cannot change once we are an adult? The answer is yes and no. We can change some things, but others are much more difficult if not impossible to alter. For example, let's say you are thirty years old. You can certainly gain or lose weight, but you cannot become taller or shorter. Alcoholics can give up drinking, and many have, but the underlying tendency to be addicted to alcohol will always be with them.

The patterns or talents we are talking about that influence our sales success are part of our hardwiring. Once formed, they are with us for life and essentially unchangeable. This is why efforts at changing some things about ourselves meet with so little success and so much frustration. These threads have taken fifteen years and hundreds of millions of stimuli to form. You cannot, for example, erase this process with a three-day course on sensitivity and suddenly become more empathetic. As far as your wiring goes, by the time you are an adult, you are what you are.

Some time ago we were doing a project for a large trucking company. This company operated a fleet of eighteen-wheelers, and they were understandably concerned about driver safety. As they pointed out to us, any accident with a semi tractor-trailer is a big deal. They hired us to help select drivers who would be more safety conscious.

We approached this assignment in much the same way we would have for companies that used us to help select salespeople. We looked at the best and tried to understand what they had in common. In this case the company identified the drivers with the best safety records. Then, we looked for questions that these drivers answered differently from the rest of the drivers. One of the questions we found most useful was: "What do you think about when you're driving?" Take a second and think about your own answer to that question.

Since it was an open-ended question, we received all kinds of answers from drivers. Some told us they thought about where they would stop for lunch, or for their overnight stay. Some told us they thought about what they would do when they finally got home. Some listened to radio talk shows and thought about whatever the topic of the day was on the show. One driver told us that he used to think about his girlfriend, but now that he was married, he didn't think about anything. As we said, we got all kinds of answers.

The safest drivers told us that they thought about what was going to happen next on the road. What would they do if the car in front of them swerved into their lane? Where would they pull over if something happened? How would they stop their trucks if their brakes failed while going down a steep hill? These were the answers that came to them spontaneously. No doubt you can readily see how such a pattern of thinking would be extremely advantageous for drivers. This pattern keeps them alert and prepared, engaged in what they are doing.

All of us who drive have thoughts like this occasionally while we're on the road. However, we found that the safest drivers had thoughts like this nearly all the time they were driving. This pattern of thinking was very pronounced in those individuals, and it was the response they gave right off the top of their heads when we asked our question. We found that driving recruits who exhibited this thinking pattern in their interview were highly likely to become safe drivers.

You may be wondering why the company couldn't just get all of their current drivers to think like their safest drivers on the road. This is a lot easier said than done. Think about your own answer to the question we posed to drivers. What do you think about when you drive? The best salespeople (yes, we have used this same question for sales interviews) often have a very different pattern. They tell us they think about their next call, or their last call. They may think of a better response to a customer's question, or rehearse in their minds what they are going to say to their next customer. They may think about how to solve a customer's problem. Or they may be on the phone with a customer.

If you think along these lines when you drive, you may be a great salesperson, but not necessarily the safest driver. You can try a little experiment. The next time you are behind the wheel, try to think only of what is going on in the road ahead of you. If you are driving in nasty weather or very heavy traffic, you may be able to think like that for a while. But sooner or later you will return to your own natural pattern of thinking. We can override our patterns from time to time when we absolutely have to, but we cannot really change them. In due course we fall back to following our most pronounced patterns. These patterns are part of our hard-wiring.

The fact that these talents, once formed, are unchangeable has profound implications for how we think about and develop strengths, and how we think about our weaknesses as well.

How Our Talents Affect Us

Every day you respond to thousands of situations almost without thinking. How do you react to the people you meet on the street? Do you automatically smile in a friendly greeting, or do you wait for the other person to acknowledge you first? Perhaps you lower your eyes in an effort to avoid any contact at all. When you sit down on an airplane, do you introduce yourself to the person sitting next to you, or do you bury your head in a book? When you bring in the mail, do you put it in a place where it will be easy to find later, or does it end up scattered around the house? If we went into your office, would we find things neatly organized, or would we find a mess? If you have a task to do that you don't like doing, do you make yourself do it right away, or do you put it off to the last possible moment?

In each of these situations your pronounced talents—your superhighways, so to speak—are hard at work. These talents filter the information your brain receives and influence the response you make. If you walk into a crowded room, you may be excited and try to meet as many people as possible. But someone else's response could be quite different. He may scan the room for a familiar face and look for a comfortable spot to spend the evening talking with close friends.

Let's take another example. When you walk into a room, what do you notice first? When we studied exceptional hotel housekeepers (yes, even in housekeepers, underlying talents were the best explanation for differences in performance), we found that they tend to notice immediately any dirt or disarray in the room.

Simply put, they see dirt better than most other people. Perhaps you have the same reaction or know someone like this. Or you may be someone who can step right over a garbage bag in the middle of the kitchen floor and not realize it was there.

If someone starts arguing, one person's response may be to become confrontational and argue right back. Another person's response may be to try to calm the person down, and still a third person's response may be simply to leave the room. These are all examples of how our pronounced talents influence our responses to situations.

Even though several people might be exposed to the same situation, such as walking into a room, they all have a somewhat different reaction. Our pronounced talents guide those reactions. The human brain develops thousands and thousands of these threads or patterns. In many respects we are just beginning to understand this process. But for our purposes, we are interested only in those patterns that can have a productive application in a particular setting such as sales or management or leadership.

When we studied hockey players, we found a pattern best described as elongated time. It seems we all perceive time a little differently, especially during a fast-paced activity. For most of us when we are in a chaotic situation things seem to go by in a blur. It's as though things are speeding up. Some people have the opposite experience, however; they seem to see things unfold in slow motion. Great hockey players often described that sensation to us. They could see the plays unfolding in slow motion. Why do their brains work like that? We don't know, but we often found these patterns.

Great baseball hitters described the same sensation. Some said they could see the ball leaving the pitcher's hand, even seeing the rotation of the ball. Most of us would barely see a ball traveling at ninety miles per hour until it was safely tucked in the catcher's mitt. But for those hitters with a pronounced pattern of elongated time, it's a different story. Small wonder they are able to hit home runs.

Literally countless numbers of patterns exist. We have uncovered a good many as we have interviewed great performers in different occupations. But patterns that have to do with hitting baseballs, singing opera, painting masterpieces, or driving eighteen-wheelers are not the patterns that are important to understanding sales talents.

Sales Themes

After many thousands of interviews and many years of research we began to see that certain themes were especially important in sales. The talents in these themes had to do with people's motivation, their ability to impact other people, the way they form relationships, the way they get their work done, and their ability to think about customers' problems.

Even with this somewhat narrower scope of themes, we still found an abundant possibility of talents. In our early work in helping clients recruit great salespeople, having so many themes was helpful in pinpointing exactly the various talent configurations found in their best producers.

After a company hired an outstanding salesperson, they frequently wanted some help in developing that individual's potential. Since potential was very much tied to talents, our clients wanted help building strengths-based organizations.

As our emphasis shifted from solely recruiting talent to developing talent, we learned some important lessons. First, we realized we needed to have a clear, understandable language. In order to build on their talent themes, people needed to understand the precise meaning of their themes and also the shades of complexity and variances that accompany their own unique talents in those themes. Consider, for example, the Competition theme. Just as the color blue comes in many shades, talents in the Competition theme also come in many shades. Since people can be competitive in very different ways, they need a way to communicate and understand what those shades are. Second, while it might be more accurate to have hundreds of different themes, having so many different definitions would become confusing. In order to help people develop their strengths, we had to have enough themes to capture their uniqueness, yet not so many that describing them would become confusing.

After carefully reviewing our database consisting of hundreds of thousands of people we had interviewed, we selected thirty-four themes that we believe accomplish both of the requirements. These themes capture most of the responses and reactions that influence performance while allowing us to describe them in straightforward, understandable terms.

Yes, there is some arbitrariness in picking thirty-four themes versus thirty-eight or forty-two. Based on a review of our data, thirty-four seemed to strike the best balance. And yes, anytime a researcher names something, some arbitrariness is involved. Shakespeare said, "A rose by any other name would smell as sweet." Of course it would. We could just as easily have given these themes other names. Bear in mind that the important aspects of the themes we have identified are not so much the actual names we have used, but rather the complete definitions or, if you will, the "smell" of those themes.

Following are the thirty-four theme names. You can find a complete definition of each theme in the appendix.

Achiever	Futuristic
Activator	Harmony
Adaptability	Ideation
Analytical	Includer
Arranger	Individualization
Belief	Input
Command	Intellection
Communication	Learner
Competition	Maximizer
Connectedness	Positivity
Context	Relator
Deliberative	Responsibility
Developer	Restorative
Discipline	Self-Assurance
Empathy	Significance
Fairness	Strategic
Focus	Woo

Missing Themes

Not long ago we were conducting a seminar about sales strengths. We had just reached the point at which we were describing the thirty-four themes when it was time to take a coffee break. During the break one of the participants came up to us, and we asked how he was enjoying the program. Usually we get comments such as, "It's terrific," or "I am learning so much." But instead this participant stared at us with something less than enthusiasm in his eyes and said pointedly, "Your list is worthless."

He went on to tell us that he had been a highly successful sales manager for more than twenty-five years. In his opinion one of the most important characteristics of a great salesperson was determination. How could we compile a list of themes or characteristics of great salespeople and not include determination?

It's an excellent question. You may be thinking of characteristics that you associate with great sales performance. Why doesn't our list of themes contain things such as aggressiveness, friendliness, persuasiveness, or organization? The answer is the same answer we gave to our participant.

Determination can be important, but people can be determined for very different reasons. In some cases their determination stems from their Discipline. In other cases it may stem from their Significance (their desire to be successful) or from their Command theme, which tends to make them more determined when they meet with resistance. So the talents found in determination, aggressiveness, persistence, and organization are all in our list. They are just part of one or several different theme definitions that make up the thirty-four. We believe it is more helpful for people to understand where their determination comes from than to simply know that they have it.

As we said earlier, we could have used other names to describe these themes. However, naming a rose a rose and a petunia a petunia is not as important as having a clear understanding of what roses and petunias look like, smell like, and feel like.

One of our goals with our clients is to help establish a clear vocabulary, enabling them to talk about talents in a consistent and clearly understandable manner. Unfortunately, the language we have to describe strengths is particularly scant. We do a much better job describing weaknesses. We all know what "paranoid," "compulsive," or "bossy" means. But so far, describing strengths is difficult and confusing for many companies and individuals.

For this reason we use these thirty-four themes to describe the talents not just of great salespeople, but also of managers, leaders, marketing people, in fact the whole gamut of business occupations. This enables the people in an entire organization to talk knowingly about each other's strengths. In a later chapter we will talk about how important it is to understand the strengths of your manager and those you work with. Understanding these themes will help you do that. Obviously, the themes that pop up as most pronounced for accountants are typically quite different from those that pop up for great salespeople.

Signature Themes

No one we have ever interviewed has had an equal amount of talent in all thirty-four themes. Nor have we ever found anyone who has no dominant themes. Moreover, we have never found anyone with all thirty-four themes highly pronounced. We can only have so many superhighways running through our brains, and everybody has some.

What we typically find is that most people have a few themes that are much more pronounced in them than in other people. You might know someone who is more competitive than anyone else you know, more disciplined than anyone else you know, or more empathetic.

We also have themes in us that are about average in intensity. We might communicate as well as a lot of other people, but it's not really something that sets us apart. Or we might enjoy being recognized for our accomplishments, but it's not a matter of life and death for us to be up on the podium receiving awards.

And we all have some themes that are barely present. We may not give a hoot about including others in our circle of friends. Or we may be reluctant to confront people when they disagree with us.

While it is interesting to know how dimly or brightly all these themes burn in you, what is most important is to understand your most dominant areas of talent. Our research suggests that this usually comprises your top five themes, which we refer to as your Signature Themes.

Your Signature Themes are your most dominant areas of talent, as compared to your talent in the twenty-nine other themes. If your top theme is Arranger, for example, it means that your talents for managing variables and properly aligning them are probably greater than your talents related to any other theme. This is one of your top areas of talent.

Knowing your Signature Themes is a key to understanding the areas in which your talents will allow you to outperform others. For salespeople it means understanding the best possible way to go about your job. This knowledge can help you develop a selling style that matches your inherent talents. And this knowledge will help you understand what the best possible sales job for you would be. Understanding your Signature Themes will allow you to focus your time and energy on those areas in which you naturally excel.

CHAPTER 4

StrengthsFinder

It seems as though our Signature Themes should be obvious to us. Don't most of us know what our underlying talents are? At the very least, shouldn't we be able to read down the list of descriptions and pick those themes that seem to be most like us? Our experience in working with many individuals tells us it's a bit more complicated than that. Surprisingly, most of us are unaware of what our own strengths are.

Our Signature Themes, the areas in which we possess our most dominant talents, are so much a part of us that they are nearly invisible, at least to us. This is true partly because almost all of us think of ourselves as normal. If we love vanilla ice cream, we assume that most people love vanilla ice cream as well. If we're well organized, ambitious, and relate easily to others, we simply assume it's normal to be that way. The more pronounced a particular theme is in us, the more it seems normal to us to be that way. And we rarely think of being normal as a talent.

Ironically, instead of seeing our Signature Themes as our own uniquely dominant areas of talent, we sometimes view others without those same pronounced themes as somewhat lacking. Artists snub those who don't understand their art. Empathetic people tend to view less empathetic people as thoughtless. "How could you have said such a stupid thing?" Mick's wife wanted to know. "Didn't you realize how sensitive she is about her new haircut?" Actually, Mick doesn't have a clue about most people's sensitivities. But Mick's wife is more likely to see that empathy is lacking in Mick, than to realize it's an especially strong area of talent in her.

People with dominant Achiever themes might view others without such dominance in that theme as lacking ambition. People who are good at meeting new people may view people without this characteristic as cold or aloof. When we have an abundance of a particular theme, we often don't think of it as an area of talent; we just think that is the way people are supposed to be.

Sometimes we see only the downside of a theme and so fail to recognize the specific talents it holds. Bill sees himself as negative. He constantly contrasts himself to several other members of the sales staff who are overflowing with Positivity. Sometimes he finds himself wishing he were more like them. But Bill is not like them; he is quite different. Deliberative is one of Bill's Signature Themes. Instead of bubbling over with enthusiasm, Bill thinks things over carefully and thoroughly. He is quick to see the downside and is usually direct about communicating possible pitfalls. Bill, without question, looks before he leaps, and this quality has saved many of Bill's customers from making expensive mistakes. Because of this quality, Bill's customers have come to trust his recommendations. It's a tremendous strength, but he doesn't see it. Like most of us, Bill is blind to his most pronounced theme.

Another reason it's hard for us to pinpoint our own Signature Themes is that we lack objectivity about ourselves. Have you ever met someone who thought she had a good singing voice but was not especially good at all? Still, after she finishes a song, everyone tells her how much they enjoyed it.

Do you think this same thing doesn't happen in business? We worked with a CEO who thought he was an excellent communicator. But this was far from true. His speeches and memos came across stilted and more often than not left his employees uninspired. His real strengths were elsewhere, but according to him, Communication was at the top of his list. He couldn't have been more wrong. To make matters worse, many of his executives told him how good his speeches were. Of course, behind his back they had a different opinion, but all this "sucking up" gave the CEO a very misguided view of his strengths. Being objective about ourselves is not always easy, and misleading feedback from colleagues can make the process even harder.

Life's Clues

Even though discovering your Signature Themes can be challenging, life occasionally offers some clues in the form of yearnings. Yearnings are those inklings of thought we have that make us believe we might be good at something, or that we might like to try something or even be something. While we are in school, we might think we would enjoy participating in debates. Maybe we've always thought we'd be good at taking pictures, or writing a short story.

It may well have been a yearning that got you to try sales in the first place. Maybe you realized that you would prefer being out and about all day rather than being chained to a desk and office. Or maybe you realized you were good with people. Perhaps you were a teacher and realized you were good at explaining things to other people but wanted to do it in an occupation that paid a lot more handsomely.

Yearnings can come at any age. Most of the salespeople we talked to had no thought of sales as a career while they were growing up. "I was a history major in college," Brian told us, "but then when I went to look for a job, I realized companies did not have history departments. They had accounting departments and engineering departments and sales departments. My brother-in-law was a salesperson for a medical device company. I thought, hey, I could do that. I learn things quickly, and I like talking to people. The more I found out about what the job entailed, the more I thought I would really enjoy it." Brian's yearnings led him to a successful career.

Yearnings also come in other forms. Do you think about living in a big house, or earning a spectacular income? Do you feel a need to receive recognition, and do you ever imagine yourself standing in front of a crowd receiving an award?

Are we saying that desiring to live in a big house or wanting to earn a spectacular income is an indicator of talent? Well, yes . . . we are saying exactly that. Wanting recognition, whether it is in the form of respect from your colleagues, living in a mansion, or driving an expensive car, is associated with the Significance theme. When this theme is very pronounced in people, it propels them to get things done. Hence, these desires—these talents within the Significance theme—are really patterns of thought that have a productive application.

They drive you to accomplish tasks in order to gain the recognition you want. Yearnings such as these can be an indication of talent.

So then, yearnings can be about either doing something or wanting something. Most of us have both kinds of yearnings. Mary wants to play the piano, and she wants to become famous as a pianist. Can you see the distinction between the first part, which is playing the piano (doing), and the second part, which is becoming famous (wanting a particular reward)? When we interviewed highly successful salespeople, we almost always found pronounced talent themes that had to do with doing and others that had to do with wanting.

An old expression says, "Be careful what you ask for . . . because you just might get it." This expression might be better stated this way: "Understand what you want so that you can go out and get it."

What do you want? What do you think about doing? What do you think you might be really good at? What do you think you would enjoy? All of these questions can help you understand your yearnings. While yearnings do not always lead you to your talents, they frequently are an important first clue.

A second clue to your underlying talents is rapid learning. The best performers in virtually every activity we have studied have gotten off to a fast start. Yes, we have found some exceptions to this rule, but not many.

By rapid learning we're not necessarily talking about passing quizzes and taking tests. Rapidly learning how to hit a golf ball is different from rapidly learning the rules of golf. Some people will start hitting golf shots a lot more quickly than others even with the same instruction and practice. Some people will learn to type much faster than others. And it is certainly true that some people have learned to sell much more quickly than others.

Sometimes we are surprised at how quickly we are able to master a new skill. When this happens, it usually means we have hit on one of our more pronounced underlying talents. We interviewed Brad shortly after he returned from a weeklong course on advanced selling skills. The very best part, he told us, was the half day spent on closing techniques. "I ate the information up, and I couldn't wait to get in front of my customers and try these new techniques out . . . and the best part is, they really work."

Most of us have heard the expression "no pain, no gain." This expression comes from the gym where weight lifters are encouraged to do repetitions until it hurts. This causes the muscle to grow stronger. We have no idea if this theory is true for weight lifting, but we do know that this expression has spawned the belief that improvements come only from great difficulty.

Nothing could be further from the truth. In most cases, if we have the right underlying talents, we are able to learn things quite easily. If we find ourselves struggling, we may be trying to learn something that requires talents we simply don't have. To rewrite a popular expression: "If at first you don't succeed, try one more time, then give it some serious thought."

Another clue to help identify underlying talents comes from satisfaction. One recurring observation we have made is the inexorable pull that the talents in our Signature Themes have on us. When we are traveling on those superhighways in our brain, we tend to feel good. As humans, we derive a sense of satisfaction when we are invoking those comfortable and well-defined patterns. In many cases our feelings of satisfaction are actually pulling us closer to our most pronounced themes. And so, these feelings are worth paying attention to. At least as far as productive activities go, we can offer some scientific basis for the expression "if it feels good, do it."

One last clue can best be described as a glimpse of excellence. Brian told us about his early days as a medical device salesperson. "I was making a presentation in front of seven or eight nurses. I could feel myself connecting with these customers. All of a sudden I realized that I could really do this job." A glimpse of excellence is not a lucky shot or a flash-in-the-pan performance. Rather, a glimpse of excellence comes when we find ourselves in the middle of a near-perfect performance, and we have a sense of how we got there and how we can get back to that very same spot again.

Glimpses of excellence are important to note. During the course of your day you'll find yourself involved in countless activities. In what activities do you find those glimpses showing up with some frequency? Sometimes the answer to that question can be surprising. Kent told us he was doing a special project for the marketing department when he realized he was doing an excellent job at pulling together all the information they had requested. "Suddenly I realized that I was much better at dealing with information than I was at dealing with people." This glimpse of excellence on Kent's part got him to apply for a sales analysis position. This turned out to be exactly the right move for Kent, and the delighted vice president of sales told us that no one was ever more perfectly suited for the role.

Mentors and Coaches

Some people have an almost uncanny ability to see talents in other people. This ability is very much a talent in its own right and is included in one of the thirty-four themes listed in Chapter 3. People with a strong Individualization thread instinctively observe other people's styles, their motivation, how they think, and how they build relationships. They naturally see what makes others unique.

Every once in a while we run into someone who can read us like a book. We may have had the great fortune of having someone like this as a teacher, or a high school coach, or a manager. These individuals are able to see things in us that may be invisible to ourselves.

Many of the great performers we have studied in sales vividly told us about having such a person in their lives. This was a person who helped them discover themselves. Lisa told us her story. "I was sitting in my office working as a computer programmer when the vice president of sales came in to see me. I'd had a few brief interactions with him in the past and he had a terrific reputation as a manager. He sat down in my office and asked me if I wanted to be a programmer for the rest of my life. I wasn't really sure how to answer. He then proceeded to tell me that I was wasting my time writing programs." (Individualizers can be quite blunt.) "'You may not have ever thought about sales,' he said, 'but you have an incredible ability to impact others. And you have one of the strongest desires to get things done I have ever seen.' He had me pegged. He seemed to know more about me than I knew about myself. So I went into sales. I have never looked back, and I know now, I am doing what I should have been doing my whole career."

Unfortunately, as you have probably found out on your own, people with a strong Individualization theme are not always around. You may well meet only a handful of such individuals in your lifetime. Nevertheless, this mentoring relationship can have a profound impact on your career.

Many companies have set up mentoring programs to

try to force these kinds of relationships to develop within their organizations. Usually the people selected to serve as mentors are simply senior managers. They may be exceptional managers, but that doesn't automatically mean they are able to identify underlying talents in others. Therefore the advice they give is hardly ever strengths based. More often than not their suggestions are the usual "get ahead" pabulum: "Do this, do that, and the next thing you know, you will be promoted. And since I am your assigned mentor, I will help you along the way...if I am still here, that is." You may want to exercise some caution in applying advice from these pseudomentors. True mentors, on the other hand, are worth their weight in gold.

Activity Analysis

Can't we just identify those parts of the job we do well to figure out what our underlying talents are? The answer is yes, but the information we glean from this process is often not specific enough to be broadly helpful. Here's the problem. Let's take an activity such as prospecting as an example. Prospecting is a common component in many sales jobs. When we analyze a sales force, it's not unusual to find some people who are great at prospecting and some who are not.

While people's performances in this activity are related to their underlying talents, no single theme is responsible. There is no prospecting theme. Remember, these patterns actually form by about the time we are three years old. Very few three-year-olds are engaged in much prospecting. They are not out looking for customers. They are still trying to get to the potty on time.

Even from the age of three to fifteen, while some of our patterns are being turned into personal superhighways, most of us are not doing much prospecting. The themes that develop tend to be more general.

While we were doing some work for one client, we interviewed a number of individuals who represented the company's best prospectors. They all performed this activity much better than their peers. But when we delved a little deeper, we found that they all accomplished this task very differently.

Mary was great at meeting new people and making a very favorable first impression, even on the phone. This talent is related to a theme we call Woo (for "winning others over"). It made setting appointments easy for her. Ted, on the other hand, had a very strong Analytical theme. He picked out those characteristics that he felt would make a customer most likely to be interested in the company's product. He used his Analytical talents to target his efforts. John had a very strong Command theme. He prequalified his customers so well on the phone that he was almost guaranteed to make a sale when he showed up for his appointment. Marty was something of a mystery to us. Marty's most dominant themes didn't seem to match those we saw in other great prospectors. Then we realized he was overflowing with Discipline talents. Even though he was not very good at prospecting, he forced himself to do it three hours every day. The end result was that he had more prospects to call on than most of the rest of the sales force.

So, while knowing that you are good at prospecting is helpful information, it is much more instructive to understand the underlying talents that influence your success in this activity. In order to develop in her job, Mary may not need to do more prospecting. What would help Mary the most is finding a way to use her Woo talents in more aspects of her sales job. Ted, John, and Marty all have a similar challenge: finding out how to use their underlying talents on a more consistent basis. But in order to do that, they need to understand what those underlying talents are.

The StrengthsFinder Profile

Uncovering your specific talents can be a difficult process. Even the first step, identifying your greatest *areas* of talent, presents a challenge. Despite the many clues life may offer, and even with the benefit of an insightful person, discovering your talents is hard. However, from our years of helping companies recruit talented salespeople we recognized that talents often surface as spontaneous responses to questions. In fact, it is one of the best ways we have uncovered to help in identifying talents.

The interviews we use to predict success in a given sales role are not easily adaptable for development purposes. These interviews are highly refined to help us uncover very selective subthemes that are common characteristics of the best performers in a *particular* sales role. This information is enormously valuable to companies in helping them select the right salespeople for their positions. These interviews were not designed to tell salespeople what the best possible role for them might be. They did not tell salespeople what their Signature Themes were. In response to this need, Gallup researchers developed the computer-based StrengthsFinder assessment.

StrengthsFinder's purpose is not to anoint you with strengths but *to find where you have the greatest potential for strengths*. Thus, StrengthsFinder measures the presence of talent within the thirty-four themes of talent that we discovered are most indicative of success.

Once you have completed the assessment, you will immediately receive your five most dominant themes of talent—your Signature Themes. These talents in these themes may not yet be strengths, but each of your Signature Themes does contain some of your greatest talents, and therefore your greatest potential for strengths.

On the reverse side of the back jacket of this book you will find a personal identification number. Log on to the Internet and go to the following address: http://www.strengthsfinder.com. Follow the instructions and, when prompted, insert your ID number. (To complete the profile, you will require a 28.8 modem or faster, and version 4.0 or higher of Internet Explorer, Netscape, or AOL.) The StrengthsFinder Web site will orient you to the system by showing you one sample pair of statements and then begin the paired statements from the assessment itself.

As you proceed through the assessment, remember that you should respond with your top-of-mind answer. Try not to analyze your response in detail. And don't be concerned if you find yourself marking "Neutral" for some of the statements. The purpose of StrengthsFinder is to isolate your most dominant themes of talent—your Signature Themes. If neither of the paired statements triggers a strong reaction or if both statements fit you equally well, then obviously this statement pair hasn't tapped into one of your most dominant themes. In either case, "Neutral" is an appropriate response.

A final word of reassurance: We have found that some people are nervous about taking the assessment because they worry that their Signature Themes will not be "good" themes. This worry is misplaced. A theme in isolation is neither good nor bad. It is simply an area of talent, and all talents are valuable in that they hold potential for strengths. When you receive your Signature Themes report, your immediate reaction to your five Signature Themes will be affected by your talents in those very themes. For example, if you discover that Activator is one of your Signature Themes, you will probably react by demanding to know what you can actually do with this new knowledge. If Analytical is one of your top five, you will immediately start to wonder how we derived this theme from your responses. Your most powerful themes will always filter your world and prompt you to react in certain recurring ways. However, no matter what your themes are, try not to react by listening to that suggestive, critical little voice that says, "Maybe you failed the test." You didn't. You can't fail StrengthsFinder because every theme contains many, many talents, and each of your greatest talents holds the potential for strength. The only possible failures would be never discovering your talents, or never finding the right role or the right partners to help you realize your strengths.

While you don't need to take the StrengthsFinder interview to read and understand the rest of this book, now would be a perfect time to take it.

CHAPTER 5

From Strengths to Fit

Excellence is a bridge that spans from understanding to application.

Read the following statement and ask yourself how strongly you agree with it: "At work I get to do what I do best every day." To what extent are you able to answer with an emphatic yes?

Gallup researchers have asked hundreds of thousands of questions over the years in an effort to understand what drives exceptional performance. We have found that a person's response to the previous statement is one of the singly most important questions we have ever posed. In just the past few years we have asked for responses from more than two million people. What did we find?

People's responses to that question link directly to their productivity, profitability, and customer loyalty measures. The more people agree with the statement, the better their performance. The implications of this finding are both simple and complex.

Just doing more of what you do best can dramatically improve your performance. That's the simple part. The more complex part is finding out how to do that in your present role, or finding another role that allows you to do that.

Earlier we mentioned Michael Jordan's performance as a basketball player and his performance as a baseball player. On the baseball diamond he just was not able to use his most significant talents. All of us have to be in the right role in order for our talents to shine. That's what we mean by fit, a close match between our job and our greatest talents.

Years ago, long before we began asking the previous question, we were struck by the observation that in every organization we studied, the best salespeople appeared to be in exactly the right jobs for them, and they usually knew it. When we interviewed top salespeople, they often mentioned this to us within the first few minutes of our conversations.

John told us his story. "After college I didn't know what I wanted to do. No job seemed really interesting to me. Then almost on a lark I tried door-to-door sales. To my surprise, I liked it. I got a kick out of persuading people to buy. But I didn't like the company much. After a while I was able to get a 'real' sales job with a legitimate company. I did okay, but the job required me to call on the same customers over and over again. You had to be careful not to push people too much or they would stop doing business with your company. I actually missed the closing pressure of my old job. Finally, after several different sales jobs I found one that was perfect for me. It's fast-paced, you go all out to get the order, and I love it." John has fit . . . and he knows it.

This chapter and the next are about improving your fit. For salespeople that means adopting a sales style that takes advantage of your greatest talents, or if you are changing jobs, finding one that is as close a match as possible to your talents.

Bear in mind that even modest improvements in fit yield big improvements in performance. This is especially true for individuals who are good performers already. Improving fit is the fastest, surest, and most dramatic way to improve your success and your job satisfaction.

Understanding Your Talents

Improving fit starts with a deep understanding of your Signature Themes and the talents you possess in them. The first step is claiming those talents. This step involves bridging the gap between your subconscious mind and your conscious mind. Regardless of whether you are aware of your Signature Themes, the patterns they contain are hard at work in your subconscious mind. Just as you breathe without thinking about it, your greatest talents are operating constantly. Bringing visibility to your Signature Themes will allow you to put these talents to work more productively because you can put yourself in situations in which they are most useful.

As a result of your taking the StrengthsFinder interview, you know the names of your Signature Themes. Now you need to understand fully what those themes mean and how they apply to you. At the back of this book, in the appendix, is a detailed description of each theme. Take some time to read each of your Signature Theme descriptions carefully.

(At some point you may want to read the descriptions for all the themes. This will give you some good insight into the makeup of other people. As you read those sections, think about which themes help explain your manager, a key customer, or a colleague at work. For the time being, though, concentrate on fully understanding your own five Signature Themes.)

As you read the description for each of your Signature Themes, have a highlighting pen handy. Each description consists of a series of insights into the talents associated with the theme. Highlight the insights that you believe are especially true about you. Two people may both have Connectedness as a Signature Theme, but because their talents within the theme are unique, they may highlight different sentences within the theme description. Everyone has a unique shade of Connectedness, so understanding what each one of your Signature Themes means to you as an individual is important.

The purpose of this exercise is to become more consciously aware of your Signature Themes, and of the individual talents or patterns within them. This will certainly take more than one reading since thoroughly discovering your talents is a lifetime process, but this first step should provide valuable insights. Frequently look over your highlighted theme definitions until you are really familiar with them. We have had many attendees at our seminars who have taken the StrengthsFinder assessment. As soon as they tell us this, we always ask what their five Signature Themes are. We're surprised how many people have forgotten them. You cannot benefit from knowledge if you forget it right away. Remember that you're dealing with patterns that are ordinarily invisible to you, so it can take a little effort to fix them solidly in your consciousness.

In order to understand these themes as researchers, we isolate them. However, the brain is not as compartmentalized as that. In a way, each theme exerts a modifying influence on the others. For example, let's take someone whose Signature Themes are Achiever, Arranger, Command, Focus, and Responsibility. Now let's take someone with a similar list of Signature Themes, such as Command, Achiever, Learner, Empathy, and Arranger. At first glance we might assume that these two individuals are quite similar. After all, they have three Signature Themes in common. While these two people might share some characteristics, they will also be quite unique. Talents modify each other. This is why human beings are so different. This is also why personality profiles that try to put people in one of four boxes are so woefully inadequate.

To the extent that you can, try to see how your themes work together. This may be difficult for some of you, as it might appear that some of your Signature Themes are inconsistent with the others. In one of the examples we used in a previous chapter, we said that we found high-producing life insurance salesmen to have both Command and Empathy as pronounced themes. It's hard to imagine that someone could be very sensitive to your feelings one moment (Empathy) and a half hour later be insistent that you sign a life insurance contract right then and there (Command). But we frequently found these two themes highly pronounced within the same person.

One of the thirty-four themes is Relator. This theme pulls people toward those they already know. Relators derive a great deal of enjoyment from being around close friends, in contrast with people with the theme Woo, who thrive on the challenge of meeting new people. Rather than being intimidated by strangers, high Woo individuals find strangers energizing, and the process of breaking the ice and making a new connection is deeply gratifying for them. On the surface these two themes might seem to be opposites. But a person could easily have one, both, or neither included in their Signature Themes.

Some popularly used personality profiles suggest that

you are either an extrovert or an introvert, or that you are either passive or aggressive. In other words, you are either one thing or its opposite. We find these characterizations much too limiting to usefully define the rich complexity of human beings. It's not unusual to find individuals with Signature Themes that pull them in somewhat different directions. Understanding your most pronounced patterns may help explain some of the conflicts you feel in your life.

Practical Validation

As you become more familiar with your Signature Themes, you will start to notice their influence in your daily life. You can help this process along. Make a list of all the activities that are part of your sales job on one side of a piece of paper. On the other side write down your Signature Themes. Now draw a line from each activity to those Signature Themes that can help you accomplish that particular task.

You may well have more than one line reaching out from a single activity to multiple themes. For example, if you wrote down planning as an activity, you might draw a line to Discipline, Focus, and Analytical (assuming those three are among your Signature Themes). A single, even simple, task can draw on multiple themes.

This exercise will help you understand how your Signature Themes come into play as you go about your job. Don't be surprised if you start to notice more plainly how these themes affect other aspects of your life. Your relationship with your spouse or family members may become clearer to you. You may understand why you are drawn to certain hobbies or leisure activities.

Make another list of moments in your life in which you were particularly successful. Once again, draw lines to those Signature Themes that may have influenced that success. As you do this, you should begin to feel the theme descriptions come to life as they move from static text to true insights about yourself. Your Signature Themes will begin to make sense to you, and you should begin to see that they really are you.

One last step in the validation process is to look for additional opportunities to exercise your Signature Themes during your daily work routine. Try to put a talent theme to the test.

This is exactly what Jack did. One of his Signature Themes is Self-Assurance. We met him at one of our seminars, and he told us about an experience he had had after he had taken StrengthsFinder. "I had a large piece of business up for grabs at a sizable plant. I was quite certain our product was the best choice for their application. While I was on a follow-up call, the pur-chasing agent told me the plant manager had decided to go with another vendor. Generally the plant manager did not see sales representatives, and he had a reputa-tion for being a bit intimidating. As I was walking out of the plant, I thought it might be time to put my Self-Assurance to the test. 'I know what I'm talking about,' I told myself, 'and I'm not afraid of any plant manager.' So I walked into his office as if I were an invited guest. He was standing in an inner doorway talking to his sec-retary. I was polite and diplomatic but firmly asked if I could have three minutes of his time to explain exactly why our product would be better for his application. He agreed, and three minutes later he also agreed to a trial offer. To say the least, I was euphoric as I walked back to my car."

As a result, Jack became convinced that Self-Assurance was a theme he could count on. In this particular case he got the sale. The more important point was that he walked into the office. From that day forward he became more willing to go up the ladder and talk to senior decision makers.

If you start to put your themes to the test, you will also become convinced that they hold talents you can count on. More important, when you understand your greatest talents, you are ready to think about fit.

Issues about Fit

"Fit" is a term commonly used and misunderstood by both companies and individuals. One of the contributors to this book tells the story about the early days of his career and his fit for a particular job.

"It was more than twenty-five years ago when I was interviewing for my first real sales job. After several unsuccessful interviews, I finally found a district sales manager who was willing to hire me, but I also had to be interviewed by his boss. This upper-level manager was going to fly in and meet me at the airport for an early-morning interview. The district sales manager warned me that his boss was very particular. After all, this was a very prestigious company. 'Don't be even a minute late, and whatever you do, look your best,' he told me.

"The evening before the interview I laid out my best blue suit, a perfectly starched white shirt, and a new tie. I did this because I was going to have to leave very early in the morning and didn't want to wake my wife. So I would be dressing in dim light. The next morning I got to the airport with about twenty minutes to spare. It was just getting light outside when I stepped out of my car and saw that I had put on one black sock and one blue sock. All I could think of was the sales manager's admonition about looking my best. This would never do. I was near panic.

"Airports back then had little more than newsstands.

But I went up to one anyway and asked the sales clerk if she had any black socks for sale. She started to laugh as she told me this was a newsstand and not a clothing store. Then she laughed even harder when she saw the ridiculous blue sock on my right foot.

"'I may be able to help you out,' she said. And she took out a pair of black pantyhose from her purse and suggested I cut them off about knee high and pull them up over both socks. It might disguise the blue sock enough to get through the interview.

"With pantyhose in hand, I raced down to the airline club room where my interview was to take place. Unfortunately, the receptionist could not locate a pair of scissors, and I was quickly running out of time. When I went into the men's room, there were no privacy stalls available so I was forced to take off my pants and wiggle into this pair of pantyhose in front of everyone who was coming in or out of the men's room. I got more than my share of strange looks, but I really wanted this job.

"When I got my pants and shoes back on, I was immensely relieved. The black pantyhose completely covered over the blue sock. I was ready to march confidently into my interview. But when I did, I was in for a big surprise. The manager had been one of the individuals who had witnessed this whole spectacle in the men's room. Although he tried to be kind, his mind was made up. He told me right away that I was simply not a good 'fit' with this company."

Less than a month later this very same salesperson managed to get a job with a competitor. Not only did he turn out to be an exceptional salesperson, but he also went on to become president of the company. It looks like the senior manager's assessment of fit was way off base. Although this story is unusual, companies' misunderstandings about fit are prevalent.

Because many companies have misconceptions about what makes a good fit, they often hire sales representatives who are not ideally suited for their sales force. You may very well be in a sales job that is not a good fit for you.

In making hiring decisions, companies frequently rely on a candidate's experience, educational background, appearance, chemistry, and track record, and in some cases even whether they are wearing pantyhose. But these criteria have little value in predicting a candidate's success. They do not measure fit.

Hence, you cannot place too much confidence in most companies' selection processes, even though they believe they are being very selective. Just because a company is willing to offer you a job does not mean the job is a good fit for you. Many companies are satisfied if they can find an average performer. And some companies actually shy away from hiring great performers. Yet simply being average is a good indication that the fit is not all it could be. Most average performers respond neutrally to the statement "At work I get to do what I do best every day." When you are not in a position to use your best talents, you hardly ever generate your best results.

When you take a job, the less perfect the fit, the more potential you are surrendering for great job performance and heightened job satisfaction. The question to ask yourself about any new job or role you are thinking about is not "Can I do this job?" but rather "Can I excel at this job?"

Just like companies, candidates themselves usually evaluate a potential job with criteria that have little to do with fit. Sales professionals often seek new jobs that are consistent with their prior experience. Why? Because that's usually the easiest way to find new jobs. In most instances, experience will help you get off to a faster start, but ultimately it will not substantially contribute to your job performance or satisfaction, unless there is a better fit in the new position. Too often, when we rely on experience, we end up trading one poorly fitting job for another one.

Some salespeople may be swayed by the income potential of a new job. In most sales jobs, however, exceptional income is attained only as a result of exceptional performance. If the fit is not right, the likelihood of ever attaining that "big carrot" is slim. In other instances sales representatives who yearn to become sales managers will take a job with a particular company in hopes of rapid advancement. Here again, few companies end up promoting average performers. If the fit is not good, your performance may never justify your being offered that promotion.

Education can be misleading. People with some medical training don't necessarily make the best pharmaceutical sales representatives. Engineers are not necessarily the best technical product salespeople, and those with financial backgrounds may not be the best people to sell financial services.

Even our interests can mislead us. We interviewed Bob when he was considering taking a job for a hospital products company that primarily sold urinary drainage bags. In most hospitals, decision making is a group activity, and lots of people need to be consulted before a sale is made. Includer is one of Bob's dominant talent themes. Talents in this theme are very useful when you need to bring people together and get common agreement. Instead, Bob ended up taking a job selling sporting goods. He told us he was a lot more interested in sports than urinary drainage. However, the job selling sporting equipment required Bob to call on owners of small sporting goods stores. His talents, however, suggested that he would be much better at selling to a group of people than to one person.

Granted, almost everyone we know has more interest in sports than in urinary drainage. But that does not mean they would be better off selling sports equipment than hospital products. Usually, liking sports means that you like to watch or play sports. Those activities are very different from selling sporting equipment. Our interests do not always tell us much about fit. We have interviewed many individuals who like cosmetics, or clothes, but they were much better suited to sell something else.

Finding Fit

How can you tell if a job is a good fit with your talents? If you have followed some of our earlier suggestions, you have already started to gain some understanding. Take another look at the sheet of paper you filled out with your daily activities on one side and your Signature Themes on the other. If you notice that you have lots of lines drawn between your activities and your Signature Themes, that's a hint that your fit may be pretty good.

Reduce your list of activities to only those elements that you associate most directly with influencing your sales results. In other words, list only the most important tasks. Once again draw lines where you see connections to your Signature Themes. If you draw lots of lines, you have another indication of a good fit. However, because fit is such a critical element, it's worth some additional attention.

CHAPTER 6

The Five Dimensions of Fit

If you want to improve your appearance, find a better tailor.

We know from our research that sales success stems from patterns of thought, feeling, and behavior that explain

- our motivation,
- the way we build relationships,
- the way we gain commitments,
- the structure we need to get our work done, and
- our ability to understand and solve customer needs.

These are the five critical dimensions of fit for a sales role. Because of this, we sometimes get asked to characterize the thirty-four StrengthsFinder themes along these lines. We actually do something like that in our selection work for sales forces, but there we use very different research tools. In selection we don't use themes; rather, we look at very discrete role-specific behaviors that can be narrowly defined and that are very specific to a particular sales role. StrengthsFinder themes are much broader than these role-specific behaviors, however, and cannot always be easily categorized.

For example, a theme such as Empathy is largely relationship oriented, and a theme such as Strategic is largely thinking oriented. But a theme such as Competition can have a very broad application. Competition might explain a person's motivation, or it might explain how that person tries to impact people as in "come on, let's have a race." Talents in the Competition theme may help form relationships. We frequently see highly competitive people band together to beat an opposing team, and form a very close camaraderie as a result. And for some people, Competition explains the way they think.

In the next section we are going to use several examples of how StrengthsFinder's themes can help you understand your dimensions of fit. The best way to do this is to give you examples of these themes at work in highly successful salespeople in particular situations. However, these are just examples. We cannot describe how every theme works in every dimension. You need to decide how a theme manifests itself in you. If Belief is one of your Signature Themes, it might explain your motivation, it might explain how you relate to people, it might explain how you gain commitments, or it might explain all three.

Motivation

We are going to look first at motivation because it is the most important dimension. The best salespeople we have studied are simply much more motivated than most of the population. And while simply being highly motivated isn't enough to be a good salesperson, it is absolutely important to have enough motivation. Even before you read this book or took your StrengthsFinder interview, you probably had a good idea of how strongly motivated you are. But your StrengthsFinder results can help you understand your particular motivation and how it applies to fit.

One of the realizations you will come to as you become familiar with your Signature Themes is that they almost demand attention. If Communication is among your Signature Themes, you are very strongly drawn to talking, writing, telling stories, or explaining concepts. If Woo is one of your Signature Themes, you love meeting new people. You will meet them on planes, in supermarket lines, or waiting in the dentist's office.

Your dominant themes are almost like an appetite, and they demand to be fed. Significance is a common Signature Theme among salespeople. In the truest sense of the word people with Significance as a dominant theme want to be recognized. They feel special and they want to be appreciated for their unique talents. They like attention and need to be viewed as credible and successful.

Kathy was just such a salesperson. Her manager made it a point to call her up at the end of every week. He praised her glowingly for her accomplishments. He often mentioned her suggestions and ideas in sales bulletins he wrote to the rest of the sales force. This attention drove Kathy to even greater performance. Her Significance theme was being fed.

When the company Kathy worked for faced some tough times, it dramatically increased the number of salespeople reporting to each manager. Kathy's manager no longer had time for the weekly phone visits or the sales bulletins he used to write. Kathy no longer received the frequent recognition for her efforts that she needed. Before long her performance began to deteriorate. A key motivational requirement was no longer being fed. When fit diminishes, so does performance.

Conrad is driven by a different theme. He is loaded with Self-Assurance and has tremendous confidence in both his abilities and his judgment. Conrad likes calling the shots. His customers know that he will give them an answer right on the spot. He will not have to call the home office five or six times just to get permission to do something. But in time, the home office started to exercise more and more control over what sales representatives could offer customers. Prices became frozen, and deal structures became fixed in concrete. Conrad began to feel more like a messenger than a salesperson. When this happens, people with dominant Self-Assurance talents lose their enthusiasm for going out and calling on customers. That's exactly what happened to Conrad.

Paul has a different theme that motivates him. Paul is driven by his Competition talents. If there is a contest, he has to win. He was an outstanding performer for more than ten years. As a result of his outstanding performance, his company moved him into a role in which he was selling to national accounts. The problem was he was the only one in the company who performed that role. Suddenly, there were no contests to win; there was no one to beat. Sure, there was always the competition from other companies, but that was not the same thing as beating his peers and being onstage every year as a contest winner. With this decline in fit, Paul no longer felt motivated.

We mention these examples to highlight how important it is to understand what your motivational requirements are and to make sure you are in a situation in which they can be met. Sometimes, as happened in each of the previous cases, you may be in the perfect job, and then something changes and you no longer have a good motivational fit. Often situations like this can be easily corrected without changing jobs. But they need to be recognized for what they are. Sometimes it may take a heart-to-heart conversation with your sales manager or other company executives to restore a good fit.

Your motivation may come from one of the three themes mentioned or another theme entirely. Some people, for example, are driven by a Restorative theme that can be described as a need to fix things. Salespeople with Restorative among their Signature Themes are often a perfect match for a territory that is badly in need of repair. However, once they fix the problems, their motivation to simply maintain the status quo may not be as intense. They get a kick out of fixing, not maintaining.

Other people are driven by their Achiever theme. These individuals have a constant need to get things done. This need never goes away; on weekends, vacations, and holidays Achievers are still driven to get something done. As soon as they finish one task, they are ready to move on to the next. In fact, they can't wait to move on to the next task. If a salesperson with a strong Achiever theme finds himself working in a sales force that is largely composed of highly competitive people, he may feel like a fish out of water. Achievers may well view contests and recognition dinners as a waste of time. The more emphasis that is placed on contests, the less they will feel they belong.

Your motivation may come from one theme or several. Look at your list of Signature Themes. Are you able to find themes that help explain your motivational requirements? Then ask yourself if these requirements are met in your current situation. Our studies suggest that 40 percent of salespeople's success stems directly from being in a situation in which their motivational needs are a good match. That's roughly twice as important as any of the other dimensions of fit.

Building Relationships and Gaining Commitments

The second and third areas to think about regarding fit have to do with people. One of the terms that irks us is "people skills." The assumption behind the phrase is that we can simply learn how to deal with others effectively. Our data point in a different direction. Although skills and knowledge are crucial to strengths building, you must first possess the natural talent for the ability. You cannot take enough courses on body language, smiling, or asking probing questions to override your inherent patterns when it comes to reacting to human beings. Since a good part of your success in sales rests on the productive relationships you can create, understanding your talents in this area is critical.

It's helpful to look at dealing with people from two different perspectives. One perspective consists of gaining rapport or building relationships with people, and the other perspective has to do with gaining commitments.

In seminars on the secrets of persuasion, we use the following formula to help explain the persuasive process:

Customer Commitment = (Content + Relationship) x Asking

In order to gain customer commitment, we have to provide some information that is relevant to the customer's needs. This is the content part of the equation. A customer's willingness to accept information is heavily influenced by her relationship with a salesperson. In essence we tend to accept information more readily from someone if we have a positive relationship with that person. This combination of information and relationship is what primes the pump for a customer purchase. But in most cases, more is required in order to turn that agreement into a purchase. That "more" takes the form of asking. Some sales books like to use the expression "closing."

The psychologist Thomas Moriarty did a study that showed that subjects were five times more likely to do something if they were asked than if they were not asked. That's why asking is the multiplier in the equation.

Many training programs have been sold to sales organizations in an effort to turn their salespeople into better closers. In careful observations we made of a direct sales force, we found that even after careful training, eight out of ten new hires were unable to ask key closing questions in front of live customers. They were able to recite them perfectly in role-playing situations in the training room, but faced with a real customer, they were unable to spit the words out of their mouths. The abilities to ask for commitments and build relationships are crucial to any successful salesperson, and recognition of how we can best perform in these areas comes from understanding our Signature Themes.

Varying sales positions have very different requirements in both building relationships and asking for the business. In pharmaceutical sales, for example, a representative will typically call on the same physicians and doctors' offices over and over and over again. There is time and opportunity to develop long-lasting relationships. Most doctors are relatively permanent fixtures in their communities, and they may stay in the same offices for thirty years or more. In this setting, content also ranks very highly, and heavy-handed closing techniques usually backfire.

Contrast that to someone selling vacation time shares. These sales representatives are likely to see their prospects once and only once. They need to be able to build relationships quickly and often need to be very direct and pointed in asking for customer commitment.

Selling industrial supplies to manufacturing plants might fall somewhere in the middle. Sales representatives may call on the same accounts year after year, but constantly changing personnel inside those plants will require them to form new relationships. These sales representatives certainly need to ask for the business, but in a way that will not close the door on future visits.

Look over your list of Signature Themes. Can you find themes that you can use constructively in the process of gaining commitments and building rapport?

In our consulting practice we have seen examples of people using the Command theme very effectively. Steven sells specialty advertising. Most of the prospects he calls on will tell him initially that they are not interested. This doesn't bother him at all. Steven is not put off by confrontation, and he intuitively recognizes that an initial no can often be turned into a yes. Steven is comfortable pushing his prospects to take risks. He will not settle for half-truth responses but challenges people to be clear and honest. This helps him get quickly at what the customer's real objections may be, and thus sets the stage for him to deal with them effectively.

Jay uses his Belief talents to gain commitments. His rock-solid conviction in the value of his products sways his customers to buy. He believes in his products so much he will not easily let his customers off the hook if they balk at buying. He would not think of recommending products to customers if he did not genuinely feel it was in their best interest to buy. His Belief theme also is the principal way he establishes relationships with people. His customers view him as dependable and quickly realize that he can be trusted. It is vitally important that Jay sells a product and works for a company he believes in completely. At times when his faith in either has been shaken, his sales results dipped precipitously.

An excellent sales manager once told us that there are two kinds of people. "One kind of person would never want to host something like a Tupperware party. They would see it as imposing on their friends, and they would never want to ask their friends to buy something just to help them out. The other kind of people are those who believe the only reason to have friends is so you know enough people whom you can invite to a Tupperware party." Sarah is definitely the second kind of person.

She is the embodiment of the expression "it's not what you know; it's who you know." To her, contacts are everything. Her Rolodex is crammed full. She relishes meeting new people, and for her, exchanging business cards is an art form. She makes an excellent first impression and is quick to do someone a favor. Instinctively she believes the phrase "I'll scratch your back if you scratch mine." Favors are not just simple acts of kindness; they are obligations to be repaid, and she is more than willing to ask for a favor in return.

Sarah uses her Woo to the fullest. She began by selling local phone service to small businesses. Because she had to meet dozens of new people every day, she needed to ask for the business relatively quickly. She always looked for opportunities to help prospects with their business problems through other contacts she had made. She was able to ingratiate herself quickly with her newfound friends (customers). She was also not shy about asking customers for referrals. In her first year of selling she produced more than the entire rest of the office.

Then her branch manager assigned her to sell to much larger businesses. She was now responsible for three huge accounts. In the first few days she met everyone she needed to meet. She quickly became bored. She was no longer able to use the talents in one of her most valuable Signature Themes. Her sales results were dismal, but fortunately she recognized what the problem was and asked for her old job back.

Positivity is another theme that is often found in great salespeople. Those possessing the natural optimism of Positivity have contagious enthusiasm. Often customers welcome them as a relief from what might be an otherwise drab and dreary day. However, there is more to this theme than simple cheerfulness. Salespeople are often able to use their Positivity talents to prod customers into action. "Come on, just do it" is an appeal to action that comes naturally to individuals with dominant Positivity talents. Their presentations may not be logical, but their irresistible enthusiasm makes them likable and hard to say no to. In some selling situations, however, with long and complicated product specifications, for example, Positivity may not be sufficient to carry the day.

Some themes in our list of thirty-four are quite helpful in building rapport. Themes such as Harmony, Empathy, Includer, and Relator are obvious examples. But themes such as Communication and Responsibility can also be part of the equation in building rapport. Relationships in business are often not quite the same as relationships in a social setting. Someone with a pronounced Responsibility theme may not be the life of the party, but in business many customers end up liking sales representatives they can depend on. If you look carefully at your Signature Themes, you are likely to find one or more that help you deal with people productively. The issue for you to consider is how you can use that talent to the fullest.

If you naturally develop deep relationships with customers, but are in a job in which you see a customer for only fifteen minutes and then never see them again, you are squandering a valuable talent.

Structure

The next dimension of fit involves structure. Talents related to structure help us get our work done. Think back to when you were in school. You may recall different study habits people had in order to do their homework. Some students found it beneficial to study in the library. Other students found the library much too distracting because they were easily diverted from their books by whatever was going on around them. These students needed to study in the seclusion of their own rooms. Still others needed to join a study group with three or four other students in order to get through the material.

We all don't work equally well in the same structure. Some people can work at home, and some people need the surroundings of an office to be productive. When we look at sales jobs, we find many different structural components. Some sales representatives are required to check in to an office every day and to check back in at the end of the day. Others may work primarily from an office and visit customers only when specific appointments are set. Still others may be working largely out of their homes with very little in the way of support. Structure relates to more than our physical surroundings. It also describes the order—or chaos—that we have to deal with.

Dominant talents in themes such as Adaptability, Arranger, Discipline, and Focus are examples that sometimes explain a person's success in this dimension. Gary works for a fast-paced company that is constantly changing its product offerings, its pricing, and even the accounts that are assigned to sales representatives. Fortunately, Adaptability is one of Gary's Signature Themes. He's able to roll with the punches very easily and reassess what he needs to do in response to the seemingly endless changes in his industry. Rather than be upset by these changes, Gary actually relishes them. His flexibility allows him to stay productive even when everything around him is in disarray.

Jennifer is quite different. She needs orderliness and predictability. She depends on routines. On Monday she knows exactly what she will be doing on Friday. Jennifer exudes Discipline. Every account penetration plan is broken down into sequential steps. Fortunately, Jennifer works for a company that operates like clockwork.

What a disaster it would be if Jennifer and Gary suddenly swapped jobs. Both are excellent salespeople, but Gary would find the orderliness of Jennifer's company tiring and would be irritated to have to deal with all of the administrative requirements. Jennifer, on the other hand, would quickly become frustrated with the lack of consistency at Gary's company.

Can you juggle many balls at once, or do you prefer to concentrate on a single objective? Do you naturally set priorities? Do you start things quickly? Do you need to complete something once you have started it?

All of these questions have to do with either the structure you bring to your work or the structure you need to have at your work. Just like other dimensions of fit, your familiarity with your Signature Themes can help you identify your talents and needs in this area.

Solving Customer Problems

The last dimension of fit involves recognizing and solving customer problems. These talents can be enormously helpful when customers have complicated problems that need to be addressed. Most sales roles do not have these requirements to a great degree.

Strategic, Input, Ideation, and Futuristic are just a few examples of helpful themes for solving customer problems. We often find that themes such as these are pronounced in great salespeople who are involved in high-level consulting, or who must develop very unique solutions for each customer.

If one or more of your Signature Themes seem to largely describe your talents in thinking, a sales role that requires a lot of mental activity and problem solving is often a better fit than one without such requirements. Great salespeople in whom these themes are dominant quickly grow bored when they must present the same material over and over again. When this happens, they find it difficult to have enough intensity about their work to generate exceptional results.

Lately it has become fashionable for many companies to refer to their salespeople as advisers, consultants, or business specialists as a way to elevate their stature in the eyes of their customers. Since customers all want to deal with vice presidents, we will just call all of our sales reps vice presidents, or so the thinking goes.

However, when we look at the day-to-day activities of many of these jobs, they are more involved in selling routine solutions for routine problems. There is nothing wrong with that. Most large businesses have become large because they have figured out a common solution that will help a majority of customers. Most of these products still need to be sold, but often do not require considerable problem solving. So, if you are looking to improve your fit in a way that uses thinking themes, be careful of taking a job just because of a title. Financial advisers, for example, can find themselves spending a lot more time on cold calls than on giving financial advice.

Other Fits

What about all the things that you would think apply to fit that we haven't mentioned? What about income, travel requirements, commuting time, whether it is a growth industry, dress requirements . . . and on and on. We are not going to dismiss the importance of any of these issues. For all kinds of pragmatic reasons they could all be "must-haves" in a job. But none of these singly or together make up a good fit. Having a high-income job with no travel and a short commute will not improve your productivity. Meeting these requirements will not turn you from a good performer into a great one, nor will it meaningfully contribute to your job satisfaction. However, even modest improvements to any of the dimensions of fit will do both.

Fit, though, is not just about what we are. It is also about what we are not. Everyone has talents, and everyone has limitations. We can't think about fit without understanding both.

Limitations and Weaknesses

Occasionally, a person who has taken StrengthsFinder and received a Signature Themes report will ask why we don't also reveal the person's bottom five themes. One reason is that we simply don't need to.

Ironically, our most pronounced talents are usually

invisible to us, but our limitations are glaringly apparent. If you want to hear about your areas of "lesser talent," just ask your spouse, or your children, or your boss. Or you can just wait until your next performance evaluation and look at your "areas for improvement."

So, you really don't need us to tell you what's wrong with you. You'll get plenty of help on that score. However, we don't believe that having limitations means there is something wrong with you, especially since we all have them. Having a limitation is not like having a disease that needs to be cured. The biggest problem with limitations is not having them, but rather the gross misconceptions we have about them. One serious misconception comes from thinking a talent is actually a flaw.

Has anyone ever told you that you are too direct, or too opinionated, or too anything, for that matter? When asked to describe their weaknesses, salespeople sometimes give us responses such as these:

I am too competitive.
I am too wishy-washy (flexible).
I am too cautious.
I am too impatient with delays.
I talk too much.
I question too much.

But looking at these "weaknesses" from a strengths perspective reveals that they are actually signs of talent.

I am too competitive. (Competition)
I am too flexible. (Adaptability)
I am too cautious. (Deliberative)
I am too impatient with delays. (Focus)
I talk too much. (Communication)
I question too much. (Analytical)

Is it possible to have too much talent? We don't believe so. But our talent themes are not equally constructive in all settings. Being highly empathetic may not be the best quality for a prison warden. Think about the physical characteristic of being tall. Your "tallness" will be appreciated when something needs to be reached on the top shelf of a cupboard; however, the same characteristic may be annoying when someone has to sit behind you in a movie theater.

Talent is always a positive resource. What counts is how you use it. In some settings a dominant talent may be a little annoying and you may need to tone it down just a bit. If a you're a highly competitive person, you may need to back off when playing games with your children. It's okay to let your children win once in a while. However, if you constantly feel the need to temper your most pronounced talents at work, that's a good indication that you are in an inappropriate role. When you are in the right role, you will constantly find ways to use the talents in your Signature Themes more, not less. That process is a significant part of developing your talents into strengths.

Having an abundance of talent, then, is not a limitation. A limitation is an absence of talent in a theme. If you're frequently in a situation in which it would be helpful or necessary to have the pronounced talents in a particular theme, then their absence becomes a weakness.

Let's see how this plays out in a real-life setting. Joe is an exceptional salesperson. He also is a terrible piano player. Even his dog gets up and leaves the room when he begins to play. Even though Joe practices, he doesn't seem to get much better. Is this a weakness? Certainly not when it comes to being a professional sales rep. Joe never has to play the piano in order to get a sale. However, if Joe decided to quit his sales job and become a piano player at a cocktail lounge, his limitation would become a decided weakness.

Relator is one of Joe's Signature Themes. Over time he develops very solid relationships with his key customers. Conversely, Woo is one of Joe's areas of lesser talent. Woo directly relates to meeting new people easily, and Joe does not do this well. This is certainly a limitation, but is it a weakness?

Joe has wisely selected a sales position in which his success depends on cultivating a few large customers and keeping them over time. He seldom has to meet new customers. As a result, his lack of Woo does not affect his performance. However, if Joe changed jobs and his new sales position required him to meet dozens of new people every day, his limitation would very quickly become a weakness.

This highlights a primary strategy for dealing with limitations. As much as possible put yourself in situations in which you can rely on your greatest areas of talent and make your lesser talents irrelevant. In Joe's current job, his lack of Woo is no more relevant than his deficiency as a piano player.

However, this is not always possible. At times your talent in a particular area might not be as pronounced as you'd like, and as a result you struggle with certain tasks. Sometimes it seems that the only answer is to "bite the bullet." Twice a year Charlene has to fill out a sales planning forecast for the next six months. "I hate it," Charlene told us. "I don't mind a little paperwork, but I have no idea who is going to buy from me six months down the road. It's a waste of time." Because Charlene does not have pronounced Futuristic talents, to her this exercise seems frustrating and pointless. But in all other respects Charlene loves her job and performs excellently. So, every six months Charlene "bites the bullet" and fills out her form.

Certain strategies can help you manage your weaknesses in a much less painful way. A support system is just such a strategy. Supplementing your talent with a support system is much like sharpening your less-than-perfect eyesight by putting on a pair of glasses.

Don's tremendous talents in Woo and Achiever enabled him to establish many new contacts with great potential as long-term customers. After each call, Don would return to his car, fully intending to fill out his call report form. But before he knew it, he would abandon the report to rush off to his next prospect. At the end of the week, when he was required to turn in the reports, Don had forgotten many of the important details of the sales calls he had made—details that were critical to his follow-up visits. Was that a weakness? Absolutely! But upon realizing and accepting that his talents in this area were not particularly pronounced, Don purchased a small tape recorder and dictated the details into it as he was driving to meet his next prospect. The outcome? Don's new support system led to many successful follow-up visits and profitable long-term customers.

Sometimes even a support system is not enough. Becky is also a top-notch sales producer. Her presentations in front of a customer make it hard to say no. Becky has Communication and Command talents coming out of her ears—but her Discipline talents are minimal. Much like Don, Becky found that her follow-up left a lot to be desired, but to an even greater extent. She loves making presentations and gets a tremendous charge when the customer says yes. But after that, she quickly loses interest—and this weakness costs her dearly in the form of many lost sales.

For Becky, though, support systems were not enough. Despite her good intentions, tape recorders and even e-mail reminders did not provide the boost that Becky's talents were lacking. Realizing this, Becky took the next step by establishing a complementary partnership. She teamed up with an inside customer service rep whose dominant talents in Responsibility and Relator produced excellent follow-up. Together they were terrific.

When an area of lesser talent interferes with performance, it is a weakness, and something must be done about it. Support systems and complementary partnerships have frequently served as highly effective strategies for great sales representatives who wished to manage weaknesses. On the other hand, we've also seen some that, although they might serve as a "quick fix" in less critical situations, do not provide the benefits of truly managing weaknesses.

One of these strategies was described to us by a sales manager. He told his new salespeople, "Sincerity is such an important part of this business that if you don't have any, you will need to learn how to fake it."

Based on our experience, faking it is not a very good strategy if you need to call on a theme over and over again in order to obtain results. But we have seen exceptional salespeople get by with this strategy from time to time in less crucial areas.

Barry is not a very good listener. "Even in school, I found it hard to concentrate as the teacher was giving a lecture," he told us. "But I also realized that it was a very bad idea to put your head down on the desk or to look obviously bored. So, I became very good at pretending to listen. I would nod my head from time to time as if in agreement, let my eyes follow the teacher as he walked around the room, and I could even recite verbatim the last twenty seconds or so of whatever he said. But I was not really listening. It was going in one ear and out the other."

Barry still finds it necessary to "fake" listening when he feels his customers are droning on and on. Usually he is thinking about what he is going to say next, or he is simply waiting for them to stop so he can continue talking himself. If Barry were to move into a role that required him to listen intently to customers in order to propose just the right solution, he would be lost. Fortunately, that is not really required in his current job. In Barry's situation, faking it—masking over a weakness rather than managing it—helps.

Can't Barry learn to become a great listener? Can't a person work on developing a weakness to the point that it becomes a strength? Is that a strategy? The answer is no. We repeat for emphasis . . . *NO*. With lots of work you can get a little better through increased skill or knowledge. Support systems and complementary partnerships can be very effective. And sometimes that's all it takes to stop a weakness from becoming a real handicap. But strengths are based on talent, and talent must naturally exist within you. Either you are talented in a particular area, or you are not—and try as you might, you cannot grow new talents.

The myth that we grow fastest by paying attention to our weaknesses is incredibly damaging. Sadly, some company development programs are built around this destructive myth, which usually comes disguised as career help. Carefully worded performance evaluations artfully divulge your greatest problem areas. Residents of faraway ivory towers have decreed that the only way to be successful is to master every competency—and that you must start with what you do the worst.

Such thinking is pervasive in almost every culture. We are preoccupied with finding out what's wrong with us and then trying to fix it. Ben, a sales trainer for a large corporation, told us, "I can't even count the number of times I have come out of a sales call with a trainee who immediately turned to ask, 'What did I do wrong?'" This is the curse of the average performer, always trying to improve a weakness. It is a never-ending task. Great performers follow a different tack. They figure out what they do right—and do more of it!

Fitting It Together

The ideal fit is a job that allows you to use the dominant talents within your Signature Themes on a consistent basis, but does not need or require management related to your areas of lesser talent. Keep in mind that a dominant talent becomes a strength when you refine it through skills and knowledge—and consistent use is a great source of both. Also remember that your lesser areas of talent become weaknesses only when you are in a situation that requires you to use them.

Being in the right role is hugely advantageous. Without question, if you are considering a new job, a promotion, or a new assignment, you should carefully reread this section in an effort to learn about what the best fit for you might be.

But you do not need to wait for a better-fitting job to apply the conclusions from our research. You can improve the fit in your present job right now. Go back to those three elements that result in a committed customer: content, relationship, and asking. Consider how your greatest talents will help you build those elements. Then build a selling style that makes full use of those talents.

The best salespeople we have studied often have very unique selling styles. We now understand why. They each have unique underlying talents. No wonder we have not found one "best" sales approach, even for a given industry. You have to develop the style that best matches your talents. If you take courses on sales technique, consider your talents as you pick and choose the suggestions that you believe will work for you. Amazingly, your talents act as a filter, and you are likely to intuitively recognize those ideas or techniques that will be the most helpful to you. Without question, the best selling style for you is the one that best uses your unique combination of talents.

If there are motivation or structure problems in your fit, you might be able to correct them. Doing so may require some help from your manager. One representative we know was outstanding, but he had absolutely no Discipline whatsoever. Fortunately, his manager was very insightful and determined. To prevent this great sales talent from going to waste, the manager began to personally provide a daily 7:00 A.M. "wake-up call" to ensure that the rep was out of bed and in action every morning. Now, that's a complementary partnership!

While this might seem like an extreme story, we have noticed that great managers are often willing to go to great lengths for their best salespeople. Great sales performers are often teamed with great managers. Great managers are the third key to exceptional performance. Strengths and fit are the other two keys. An exceptional manager can discover and develop your strengths and can do a lot to make a good fit even better.

CHAPTER 7

The Manager Effect

Get what you need.

Do you have the manager you deserve? For far too many of the world's best salespeople, the answer is a definite no.

In Chapter 2 we talked about many of the myths that misguide companies as they make critical decisions about who will represent their products and services. However, the most harmful myths of all might be these:

- Anyone can manage.
- Our best salespeople are likely to be our most effective sales managers.

What damage the acceptance of these assumptions does! Certainly, while there can be an overlap between those talents that lead to sales success and management success, that correlation is more rare than common. In fact, in many sales arenas, the talents that can contribute to fabulous success can inhibit managerial effectiveness, particularly if other strengths are lacking. Will that highly competitive, confrontational, independent representative be the boss of your dreams? Highly unlikely, unless she has some inclinations to invest in others and take delight in their successes, and perhaps some perceptiveness that can help her know when to tone down her directness a bit.

We were doing some work with one of the world's largest software companies. Our research with this organization's U.S. subsidiary indicated that its sales force was one of the least committed segments of its employee population. This is hardly a result that any company leader wants to hear.

As we looked into the causes, we found that many of the sales managers we talked to had excuses for this poor showing: greater competition, the increasing "virtualness" of the regional sales offices, reorganizations—an all too familiar litany of excuses for poor management practice. However, in each of the twenty-seven meetings we held with this company's various managers, we heard from at least one who, despite the increasing number of obstacles, worked hard at getting his people to stay committed and to sense that the organization cared about them.

Later, we heard from an account executive lucky enough to work for one such manager. Steve told us that he had been lured by the siren song of the dot-com craze and quit his job with the company. "I handed my resignation to my boss, John, and he told me that he knew that this move was not right for me. But all I could see were dollar signs and stock options."

Lo and behold, John was right, and Steve, after just two weeks at his new job, couldn't believe the mistake he had made. One day John called him to see how things were going, and Steve swallowed his pride and opened up. "Why don't you stop by the office on your way home tonight?" asked John.

That night, as Steve started to complain about the madhouse he'd signed on with, John opened his desk drawer and took out Steve's resignation. "I never sent this to headquarters and haven't told anyone there, including payroll, that you've quit," said John. "You can come back on Monday as if nothing has happened." Steve did just that and two years later is praying that John never retires. He has come to realize that managers like John are rare. We have noticed that great managers find a way to bend over backwards for their people at just the right time.

Is this the kind of boss that *you* deserve? How can you assure that this is the type of relationship you have with a manager?

Our research indicates that for every manager like John, there are at least four with far less ability to motivate and inspire loyalty. While we have heard a fair share about truly rotten managers, we are even more worried about the wider ranks of average bosses out there.

Bad managers tend not to stick around in good companies. They have only a short time to wreak havoc, and before long they are history. Average managers have a longer shelf life. If they have mastered any managerial skill at all, it's that of surviving. However, their impact on top producers can be just as demotivating and corrosive as that of bad managers.

Think back for a moment to your best manager. Is there any doubt in your mind that you were more productive working for that individual? Assuming the job was a good fit, you probably sold more and were a lot happier as well. You probably learned a great deal, felt committed to your role, and were more likely to be loyal. Indeed, great managers make a big difference and are the third common denominator, along with strengths and fit, we find when we study the world's best salespeople. Yet the role managers play is frequently overlooked and underappreciated. This is because of two prevalent, but largely erroneous, ideas about the way sales forces work.

The Lone Wolf

Sales representatives often work alone. They may go days or even weeks without checking into an office. The only contact with their managers for months at a time may be limited to an occasional phone call, voice mail, or e-mail. Even if they work in a crowded office, sales can be a lonely profession. They are constantly evaluated by the numbers they post each week, month, or quarter. If they're having a slump, that crowded office can seem like a desert island, with no one coming to rescue them.

So, we were not surprised to find that the best salespeople are substantially more self-reliant than those in other jobs. They are able to put up with the loneliness that often accompanies sales. More significantly, the best take full responsibility for their results, even when other factors affect their performance. Competitive products, changes in the marketplace, and even a company's ability to ship its products on time can have a huge impact on sales numbers. However, in the final analysis, the best sales reps realize that results are up to them, even when their companies are getting in their way or having a bad year.

Tim expressed it this way: "Every company has its ups and downs. Sometimes we've got the hot new product, and sometimes it's our competitor. Sometimes we have delivery problems, and sometimes our competitor does. But even in a down year, the best salespeople will still be on top. That's my goal every year. I can't stand going to a sales meeting and being at the bottom of the pack. And I can't stand people whining about every little problem. To me it just sounds like a bunch of losers making excuses. Things are never perfect, but in the end it's up to you."

This is the kind of ownership of results we hear from great sales reps. While it is helpful for salespeople to have this attitude of self-reliance, it can also mask over the important role managers play in contributing to exceptional outcomes. Contrary to popular belief, sales is not a "lone wolf" occupation. The best performers do not "go it alone." Whenever we find truly great sales performance, we usually find a great sales manager standing closely in the shadows.

Your manager can and does make a big difference—positive or negative—in how well you perform. We have followed countless individual sales representatives over the course of many years, during which time most had several changes in their immediate supervisors. When they were working with outstanding managers, their sales performances shot up, but when less able managers took over, we often saw their sales performances decline. In sales, managers make a difference! Just as legendary movie directors elicit better performances from actors, great managers can enhance sales performance. The right manager can turn talented salespeople into fully engaged employees who are much more likely to generate increased productivity. But more than that, these sales reps feel better about their jobs, are less frustrated, and are more in tune with their company's purpose. Importantly, they generate considerably more customer loyalty than other reps. Before we explain how that happens, however, we need to discuss one other myth.

The Preference Myth

When we talk to salespeople about their managers, one word in particular almost invariably creeps into the conversation. That word is "like." "Yes, I like my manager," Mary Ann told us. She went on to describe all the manager's likable qualities. By her description we're sure that he was a very nice fellow, a fine humanitarian, and a fun person to invite to a party. But none of that has anything to do with what we mean by a great manager.

The best manager you ever worked for might very well not be the one you liked the most. Liking your manager is not a bad thing, but it won't improve your productivity. Some of the best managers we have encountered were not all that likable. Some were gruff. Others seemed aloof. Still others certainly could be considered demanding. Yet these managers produced outstanding results and were able to retain their star producers year after year.

Don't get us wrong. Being gruff or aloof is not the secret to being a great manager either. Every manager has his or her own style. Many management books try to elevate one style over another. This in our view is dead wrong. We are not talking about stylistic differences here. Sure, you probably like some styles better than others, but the most important question you can ask about your manager has nothing to do with style or whether he makes a nice dinner guest. The most important question is: Is he improving your results?

As it turns out, that's a more complicated question than whether you like him or not. In order to answer that question fully and fairly, there must be some understanding of what exactly great managers do. How do they influence results? How do they improve productivity? Quite frankly, we wanted to know the answers to those questions ourselves.

The Evolution of Q^{12}

Of course, we thought we knew something about what a productive workplace looked like and what productive managers did. For years we have gone into companies and performed employee attitude surveys. We measured how people felt about everything from pay plans to parking spaces. We encouraged managers to conduct 360-degree feedback sessions. To our surprise and our dismay most companies reported that they were worse off after they completed these surveys. We had accumulated piles of data, but the data did not tell us what was different about great managers.

We began to gain some clarity only after doing a great deal of research and analysis. To that end, Gallup asked one million employees over a hundred questions each and evaluated their answers. We found that many of the questions we had traditionally asked had nothing to do with important business outcomes. So, we began to focus only on those questions that correlated to improved productivity, profitability, customer loyalty, and employee retention. We found *only* twelve questions that influenced these performance measures.

We also found that the CEO and other senior executives do not set cultures within companies to anywhere near the extent we had assumed. Cultures were not the result of company barbecues or reporting the latest bowling scores in the internal newsletter. Instead, we found that in many respects all managers create their own cultures within their work groups. These twelve items turned out to be the best ways to evaluate those cultures.

Sales managers who did a better job in these twelve areas achieved 56 percent higher attainment of customer loyalty. They also achieved 38 percent higher results in productivity and 27 percent higher results in profitability and had 50 percent lower turnover rates than managers who did poorly in these twelve areas.

Let's take a look at what these twelve all-important items turned out to be.

1. I know what is expected of me at work.
2. I have the materials and equipment I need to do my work right.
3. At work I have the opportunity to do what I do best every day.
4. In the last seven days I have received recognition or praise for doing good work.
5. My supervisor, or someone at work, seems to care about me as a person.
6. There is someone at work who encourages my development.
7. At work my opinions seem to count.
8. The mission or purpose of my company makes me feel that my job is important.
9. My associates or fellow employees are committed to doing quality work.
10. I have a best friend at work.
11. In the last six months someone at work has talked to me about my progress.
12. This last year I have had opportunities at work to learn and grow.

You will notice that we have phrased these items as statements, not questions. This is because in our research work we present them as statements and then ask participants to rate their responses to the statements from strongly disagree to strongly agree.

Some of these statements may surprise you. "I have a best friend at work" is one that usually raises eyebrows. Yet the data are very clear. People who have a best friend at work tend to be more engaged, productive, and customer focused in their jobs than people who don't. In the end, it's not that we thought these were the right questions; it's that these questions correlated consistently to outcomes. Overall, these questions measure how engaged sales reps are in their work. "Engaged" is a combination of how motivated, excited, interested, dedicated, committed, and satisfied people are in their day-to-day activities.

How engaged are you? You can take a simple test. Write down either a yes or nor for each of the twelve questions. Write yes only if you *strongly* agree with the statement, write no if you don't . . . and yes, be honest!

Now, simply add up your number of yes answers. The more you have, the more likely you are to be engaged in your job. The very best salespeople we have studied often have over nine yes answers. If you have fewer, don't feel bad. This score is more a reflection of your manager than of you. But you can do something about it.

Clean Up Your Environment

These Q^{12} items really describe the environment in which you work. Your direct supervisors or managers have the biggest influence over that environment. In many respects, they create the culture of their work groups much more than anyone else within the company. At times in your career you probably have been fortunate to work for someone who did a good job in these twelve areas. Conversely, you've probably been less fortunate at other times and, based on our research, at those times you probably saw your own performance suffer.

You are more likely to change jobs or consider what your next career move should be when you are working for poor managers. When top performers leave a company, 70 percent of the time it's because of a breakdown in the relationship with their managers. That breakdown is directly related to the twelve areas. As your scores go down, you are no longer getting the most out of your talent, and often that can be a frustrating experience. Again, it's not a matter of liking or disliking your manager, but whether that manager provides what you need. Your engagement has more to do with the encouragement, support, and involvement you receive around those twelve important workplace conditions. Consequently, the fewer yes answers you have, the greater the likelihood of your leaving. Even if you stay, your productivity is diminished.

In many cases, leaving your current job, even if you are frustrated, is not a particularly good option, especially if you really like working for the company and your day-to-day activities are a good fit with your talents. Is there anything you can do in such a situation? Yes. You can train your manager!

We were surprised to find how many great sales performers have found it necessary to do this over time. "When I first got hired," said Ann, "I worked for a terrific manager. She was really the reason I came to work for this particular company. But after a few years she was promoted to another job. Her replacement couldn't have been more unlike her. I was miserable. Finally, I had to sit her down and tell her what I needed from her. She never became a really great manager, but after that point, life at least was a lot easier for me."

Eventually, as is often the case, Ann's "bad manager" also moved on, and much to Ann's delight, she began reporting to a great manager again.

When we looked at the performance of Ann's second manager, we realized that she was a long way from being "bad." She was simply average. But we have found that having star sales performers report to average managers can often create very unhappy situations. Average or mediocre managers tend not to manage stars very effectively.

You would think that every manager would want a sales district packed with star performers. In fact, when we interview sales managers, they tell us this is exactly what they want, but the reality is quite different. Many managers would be more than happy to have a group of average performers who never cause any problems, even if they produce somewhat less. Stars, on the other hand, often cause all kinds of "problems" and usually take more time to manage.

Connie put it this way: "Sure, Kevin sells a lot, but he causes me his share of headaches. He is always on the phone asking for special pricing, or faster delivery times, or some other special request. It's as if I have nothing better to do than sit around and constantly do him favors. Tom, on the other hand, never causes a problem." Tom, we later discovered, sold only about half as much as Kevin.

In fairness we must say that Connie, as a manager, has never had any help in understanding how to handle star performers. Nor does she probably have a clear understanding of how much more people at the top sell. Even more important, she may not realize that nearly all customer loyalty comes from top performers.

The important thing for you to remember is that you can improve your own performance by helping your manager understand what you need. You can improve your own environment.

In working with many sales managers, we have become wary of the managers who continually talk about their need to have "good team players." Many of them will quote the old saw "There is no 'i' in 'team.'" No, we're quick to add, but there is an "i" (and let's make that a capital "I," thank you) in "wIn." When asked how they would manage top sales performers who are prima donnas, all too many managers tell us they would work to change them or get rid of them.

Where to Start

As you start thinking about your responses to the twelve questions, keep in mind that they are listed in a specific order for a reason. The questions can be viewed as a pyramid, with the questions that need to be addressed first at the bottom.

This last year I have had opportunities at work
to learn and grow.

In the last six months someone at work has talked
to me about my progress.

I have a best friend at work.

My associates or fellow employees are committed to doing
quality work.

The mission or purpose of my company makes me feel that
my job is important.

At work my opinions seem to count.

There is someone at work who encourages my development.

My supervisor, or someone at work, seems to care about me as
a person.

In the last seven days I have received recognition or praise for doing
good work.

At work I have the opportunity to do what I do best every day.

I have the materials and equipment I need to do my work right.

I know what is expected of me at work.

This pyramid represents *a hierarchy of employee engagement*. You need to pay attention to the questions at the bottom of the pyramid, which address employees' more basic needs in the workplace, before those at the top.

Your score means more than simply arithmetic. If most of your yes answers are at the top of the pyramid but you have a lot of no's at the bottom, you are likely to be quite frustrated in your job. For example, if you have lots of opportunities to learn and grow but don't know what is expected of you, or lack the materials necessary to do your job, your high ratings in the "learn and grow" category will be of little real value. When we see such a pattern within a sales force, we warn the company that it has built a beautiful exit ramp or that it is quite effectively training its competitors' next recruits!

In the following pages we will explore these questions in more depth. The emphasis is on what you can do to improve your environment in these areas. After all, you don't just exist in an environment; you help shape it.

1. **I know what is expected of me at work.**
   Sales organizations usually communicate expectations more clearly than most other departments within a company. You probably have a sales budget for the year. Your budget may even be broken down by lines of business or product groups. But during the course of the year many events can happen that might change these expectations. Sometimes product problems arise, or a competitor is unable to ship all their orders, creating an unanticipated opportunity. Any of these circumstances can be points to reinitiate a discussion about expectations.

   Many organizations have expectations beyond simply the sales numbers. Expectations for you can range from profit goals to keeping your company car neat. Your organization might expect you to dress a certain way during sales calls. It also might have expectations about how you conduct yourself with your customers or how you work them through a prescribed sales process. Some companies go still further. They may expect a certain number of sales calls per day, or have a featured product each month they want you to spend time against.

   Obviously, not all of these expectations are equally important. Some managers are not good at communicating expectations and priorities or helping their people sort through what might seem like a list of conflicting goals. Often we hear comments about managers layering one expectation on top of another without any real thought as to whether they can all be met or what's most important.

It is critical for you to make sure expectations are clearly spelled out and to resolve what you perceive as conflicts in your goals. Understand that sometimes mediocre managers ask for things they don't really want. One CEO told his organization he wanted his company to be "the most respected company in our industry." What he really wanted was to be the fastest growth company in his industry. His lack of clarity caused lots of turmoil in his organization.

We worked with two high-tech companies who in similar fashion were mismanaging some of their very best people. As these companies watched their businesses become increasingly complex, they elevated their best sales reps to "relationship managers." Selling these top people on this new position, the companies told them that they would have the luxury of taking the long view, of cultivating accounts so they could increase their organizations' footprints within these key clients.

Both of these high-tech giants quickly frustrated these groups when the sales managers over them demanded quarterly results, as they always had. Quickly their "cultivation" mind-set turned to a "transaction" mind-set; nothing had really changed for these high fliers. The result: frustration and many resignations.

Sometimes you have to pin your manager or your company's top executives down and find out exactly what they *really* mean. Ask them who they consider to be the best performers in the role they are offering you and investigate the numbers that those people are hitting. More than anything, this will tell you what the goals for the position truly are.

If you have a no on this question, you may want to write down exactly what you think the company's expectations are. Do you know what is expected of you not just this year but this month, or this week? Find an occasion to review this list with your manager. If circumstances change, review the list again. Having clear expectations is one of the fundamental building blocks of a good working environment.

2. **I have the materials and equipment I need to do my work right.**
The materials and equipment list generally falls into two areas. The first area is operational—those resources and "things" we absolutely need in order to do our jobs. The second area has more to do with status or the quality of relationship we have with our managers. Do we have the newest laptops? Do we get new products first? What does this have to do with relationship? If our manager intervenes on our behalf to get us these little extras, it makes us feel important, and that affects our performance.

Clearly the first place to start is with the operational items. Too many managers divide resources equally. They have a mistaken notion of fairness. Everyone gets the same sample allocation, the same expense allocation, and the same office assistance. The simple fact is that people who are performing better usually need greater allocations.

Ed told us this story: "At the end of last year the whole company was missing its sales number. As a way to conserve expenses, we were all told not to make any out-of-town sales calls for the last six weeks of the year. I have a large travel territory, so for me that was the kiss of death. But what really griped me was treating the best performers the same as people who had not sold much all year. Why not take the expense money away from them and give it to the top producers? They don't seem to mind sitting home anyway!"

The solution—potentially—is simple: If you are not getting what you need, ask for it. In Ed's case, he used his previous results as leverage and asked for additional expense money so he could continue making sales calls. Finally, his manager agreed. Great managers instinctively give more to those who produce greater results. Average managers sometimes need a little nudging. Poor managers are most likely to adhere strictly to policy and to perceive "fair" treatment as "equal" treatment. You must instruct sales managers that the only way to truly have "fair" treatment is to give the best what they deserve.

The second area of needs has more to do with ego than necessity. That doesn't mean it's unimportant. People shouldn't care how big their offices are, but they do. What kind of room you have at your national sales meeting may seem unimportant, but if you're a top producer, you may feel you are entitled to little bit more. If these accoutrements are not important to you, forget about them. However, if you are producing great results and feel constantly snubbed, have a conversation with your manager. If the lack of these special extras bothers you, it's probably affecting your performance.

Last, don't be afraid to invest in yourself. When cell phones were relatively new, one salesman told us how he tried to get his manager to pay for one. His manager balked at the idea. In the end the salesperson just decided to buy the phone himself. Eventually, the sales manager realized how much more productive the salesperson was because of the phone and authorized the expense.

One very productive rep we know has a large territory that requires occasional air travel. This rep absolutely hates to fly coach. He is larger than average, and no doubt the seating arrangements in coach are a little cramped for him. But the biggest problem was trying to fit his ego into a coach seat. Although he complained routinely to his supervisors, they were unwilling to authorize first-class air travel.

Finally, he just decided to pay for the upgrade to first class himself. While it certainly cost him a few dollars, he became much more willing to make trips to faraway customers, and his additional commissions more than made up for the expense. And, he felt better about himself. Moral of the story: If something is really bothering you and you can't get your company to fix it, fix it yourself.

3. **At work I have the opportunity to do what I do best every day.**
Fundamentally this is a question about talent and fit. More than any other question, this deals with whether you are in the right job in the first place. Whether or not you are, many minor adjustments can be made to make use of your talents more frequently. We often find the administrative requirements within many sales jobs increasing. Yet few people pursue a career in sales so they can do paperwork.

A great manager will notice that the "administrivia" is getting in the way of reps and take steps to remedy the situation. If you do not have such a manager, you might need to come up with some creative solutions yourself. How do you do this?

If you have already taken the StrengthsFinder interview and read the chapter on fit, you have a good start. What is it you do every day that really lets you use your signature strengths? Now find a way to do more of those activities. Find some ways to spend less time doing other tasks. One sales rep we know hired his teenage daughter to complete his paperwork and expense reports so he could spend more time in front of customers. Sometimes finding someone else to team up with can be the answer. Good prospectors sometimes team up with good closers or good "farmers" who can tend existing accounts well and grow them. Another rep convinced his company to hire a technical training person to train new customers on the equipment so he would not have to take time out from making new calls.

The point here is a simple one: The more time you spend every day doing what you do best, the more engaged you will be in your job.

4. **In the last seven days I have received recognition or praise for doing good work.**
Some managers are stingy with praise. One manager told his salespeople, "If I haven't yelled at you, then you're doing okay." However, most of us need more than silence to feel good about our work. But because sales is among the most solitary occupations, sales managers can be unaware of the many victories you might have had during the week. You can do something about this.

"Every time my manager called me on the phone," said Tamara, "I felt like he was in such a big hurry. But it was important to me to review the highlights of my week. Sometimes this included gaining an important piece of new business. But sometimes it was just handling a difficult account. But I realized if I didn't tell my manager what I was doing, he had no real way of knowing."

Roger took another tack. Every week he wrote down an "accomplishments list" that consisted of the things he had done during the week of which he was especially proud. It was not a big deal and took him only a few minutes. He sent the list to his sales manager every week with his call reports, and before long his sales manager began commenting on it. For Roger there was an added benefit to his approach. Reviewing our victories is a tremendous way to reinforce our talents and can be a springboard for growth.

It's very hard for managers to offer sincere praise if they are unaware of your accomplishments. For most top sales performers, praise is not something they're satisfied getting once a year or once a month. It has to be ongoing and frequent. "Don't hide your light under a bushel basket" is as good advice today as it was two thousand years ago.

5. **My supervisor, or someone at work, seems to care about me as a person.**
   Guess what? Few humans beings like going through life as a number. Sales is a risky situation in many companies. Intuitively we understand that our future is tied to our performance. If our performance suffers too much, we are toast, but nonetheless, we need to feel that we are more than just last month's sales results.

   In our leadership seminars we ask participants to fill out a personal board of directors chart. We ask our attendees to fill in the names of people whose opinion about them is important. Who are the people sitting around your board?

Not surprisingly, people usually list close family members. Their parents, their spouse, and their children are usually at the table. Often people list a minister or best friend. But almost always, even if reluctantly, people list their boss as someone whose opinion counts.

As a sales representative, you probably have well-above-average relationship talents. Use those talents to cultivate a relationship with someone at work who cares about you as a person. If it's your direct manager, so much the better. In our phone interviews we frequently found people who maintained a strong relationship with a former manager even after they no longer reported to that person. That relationship often took the sting out of reporting to a mediocre manager and helped the salesperson to maintain high performance. We do better in an environment where someone cares about us. Caring is a two-way street. You can start the process by finding someone you care about.

What should the relationship with your manager be like? We are not suggesting that you should hug or sing "Kumbaya" together. However, you need a relationship with your manager that fulfills the following requirements:

- It is intimate enough to assure that his intentions are clear. You have to know, when he talks to you, "where he is coming from."
- It is important enough to you to assure that his expectations for you are motivational rather than onerous. When people we don't know ask us to do something, we might wonder why they are asking, or what right they have to make the request. With

relationship, expectations are seen in a very different way.

- You can grow. Human beings are genetically programmed to learn in relationship with others. Without relationship, many of us learn far less effectively.

Whether that relationship is close or at arm's length, "professional" or "personal," will depend on the personalities of both you and your manager. However you "relate," the previous criteria will assure that the relating is more productive for you, your manager, and your organization.

6. **There is someone at work who encourages my development.**
One reason best performers get to the top and stay there is that they enjoy the process of getting better. This seems to be true in many professions. It's what drives the best musicians to rehearse for hours on end, or what makes a golfer practice a putting stroke to perfection. Having someone who encourages this effort fuels the process, which is why the best performers retain coaches in many fields.

This is true in sales as well. With the right talents you can learn to get better and better. However, this process seldom happens as a result of formal training. Rather, it seems to be a combination of learning events that can be considerably different for each of us. Some get better by watching others. Some get better by reading books and articles. Some get better by trial and error. The exact process is unimportant.

What is important is that we tend to do more of it when someone encourages us at work. Often this person is our manager, but it doesn't necessarily need to be. Not all managers are good mentors. Sometimes average managers are stymied at how they can help great sales representatives get better. Realistically, you may be a much better salesperson than your manager is, and he may feel uncomfortable making suggestions.

We encourage you to find someone at work who might fill this role. It could be a former manager. It could be someone else in the company who has taken some interest in you. Whoever you choose, it should be someone who sees your potential and sees a way to boost it.

7. **At work my opinions seem to count.**
Some managers do an excellent job of seeking out opinions. Pat told us he really enjoyed working with his manager because he was always asking what he thought about company issues. "He always wants to know what I think about a new brochure, or a new product, or a new competitive entry. Frequently, he writes down my comments. And he often uses my comments in his sales bulletins."

It's a great feeling to know someone cares about your opinion. It's just another way of saying, "You are important to us."

Sometimes, however, managers, especially average managers, can be intimidated by this process. Frequently, great salespeople express opinions in the form of demands. "We need to improve this product," or "We need more pricing authority," or "We need a bigger sample allocation." These demands can seem daunting to managers who are unsure how to handle them and feel unable to accommodate them. Consequently, many average managers hesitate to ask people what they think. They don't want to deal with the issues that may be raised. Their view is that sales reps should be seen but not heard.

If you find yourself in such a situation, look for constructive ways to express your opinions. You might want to make a list of your most important points. Take some initiative and write a memo or note on your sales call report. But make sure you express yourself.

Sometimes it's easier to focus on problem areas when it comes to our opinions. Give some thought to some areas that are going really well and make a point to express yourself about those as well.

8. **The mission or purpose of my company makes me feel that my job is important.**
While the goal of every company is to make a profit, few companies have that as their only goal. Often companies are quite articulate about these other goals. "We want to feed the world" and "We change the way people think" are examples of companies' mission statements. Ideally, a mission statement broadly focuses on a company's nobler purpose for being.

Are you hawking stocks, or are you helping people build financial security? Are you pushing food or providing nutrition? Mission gets at more than just believing in the product and service you are selling. It has to do with the company's reason for existence and the role you play in realizing that noble goal. Great managers do an excellent job explaining the company's mission and reinforcing the company's values. When these values are closely aligned with your own, you can be more deeply motivated, which can greatly enhance your productivity.

Make it a point to understand your company's mission. Does the company have values you personally believe in? Do you see your company providing a benefit to society at large? Are you proud of your role in accomplishing that purpose? Some of the best salespeople seek situations in which they can answer yes to each of these questions.

9. **My associates or fellow employees are committed to doing quality work.**
This is more of an assessment question than something you can directly control. As mentioned earlier, you should and must depend on others to realize your potential. If the products don't work, or they are not shipped on time, or other frequent problems hamper relations with your customers, your performance suffers in two ways. First, you lose sales directly as a result of these problems. Second, your effort will subside because your motivation decreases. If you begin to sense a real difference between your attitude about quality work and that of others in your workplace, a careful appraisal of your job situation is in order.

Don't be hasty about short-term problems, however. Often it pays to give good companies a chance to straighten out these areas. But don't be silent about them either. Make known as diplomatically as you can how these problems are affecting your customers.

10. **I have a best friend at work.**
Empirically, the data are very substantial on this point. People are more productive when they have a best friend at work. The more important point is, it does make a difference, and it's something you can effect yourself.

Don't be afraid to form close personal friendships with people at work. While conventional wisdom discourages some managers from becoming friends with those with whom they work, the very best managers behave differently. They are not afraid to form close personal relationships, and they know how to use those friendships to improve good performance rather than excuse nonperformance. If you don't have a close personal friend at work, find one!

11. **In the last six months someone at work has talked to me about my progress.**
   Too often we confuse progress with promotion. For many people progress is *not* being promoted to sales manager. Progress really has to do with getting better at the job they are currently doing. (Notice that the word is "progress"—how I've grown— rather than "performance"—how I did.) Ideally, the person you should be talking to about your growth is your direct supervisor. But just as we discussed in question five and question six, if it's not your manager, don't hesitate to seek out someone else who is interested in your development.

   Once we begin to feel that we are simply standing still, we begin to experience a sense of stagnation. This sense of stagnation starts to have an eroding effect on our performance and on the inherent satisfaction we derive from our job. While perhaps some people can evaluate their progress completely on their own, most of us need to have someone who plays the role of coach. We benefit by having someone to review our progress.

12. **This last year I have had opportunities at work to learn and grow.**

One of the biggest issues we see with companies is that much of their training and development dollars are directed in the wrong areas. Rather than taking the best performers and trying to make them better, too often training programs are aimed at poor performers and focus on what they do the worst. Unfortunately, such programs rarely accomplish much except to frustrate everyone involved.

Salespeople who are already good closers will learn and develop much more by attending seminars on closing techniques than poor closers ever will. Too often companies believe that there's no real reason to send its best performers to seminars. You might have to counter this all-too-common corporate tendency by designing your own learning opportunities or working with your manager on a meaningful or even inspiring personal development plan.

As you think about your own areas for learning and growing, think about your Signature Themes. Think about what training or experiences would complement those talents. Seek to make them happen, either inside or outside the company. Take responsibility for your own development. Be willing to invest in yourself. Improvement in your strongest areas will enhance not only your sales performance, but also the day-to-day satisfaction you gain from your work.

Whose Job Is It?

The best managers we have studied almost invariably understand their role in creating a culture in which these twelve conditions are effectively addressed. Further, the best companies assist their managers in creating and maintaining such environments.

However, as all too many people know, not all companies and not all managers do this equally well. Even if you work for a great company, at some point you'll work for a very average manager. The need for great managers far outstrips the supply. And as we will see later, many people who go into sales management really shouldn't.

During these times pay close attention to the twelve areas discussed in this chapter, and even request what you need to improve your own environment. Often this is a better approach than changing jobs, especially if it's a company you really like and it's a good fit with your talents.

You may not always have the manager you want, but you can do a lot to make sure you get the management you need.

CHAPTER 8

Building Customer Engagement

In the new millennium customer engagement is where it's at.

How many customers are satisfied with you and your company? How many of those customers are engaged? How do great salespeople develop engaged customers?

Even if you could honestly say that all of your customers are extremely satisfied, you might not be doing a good enough job. Gallup's research demonstrates that customer satisfaction is merely the foundation for a continuing relationship with customers. As a result, "satisfaction" is an unreliable standard for gauging the strength of your relationships with customers. Customer satisfaction is simply the entry point for achieving a deeper foundation that rests on total customer engagement.

One of any company's most important assets is its customer base. Taking a closer look, we find that engaged customers are the most valuable part of that asset. Therefore, your real value to your company as a salesperson is not just generating sales, but generating loyal, engaged customers. The payoff for companies is enormous: A base of engaged customers assures sustained, profitable growth—predictably. The payoff for you can be enormous as well. Engaged customers become advocates for you and what you sell. Business with such customers is often at higher margins. And, engaged customers often help you sell other accounts.

What leads to customer engagement? Is it products, marketing, service, follow-up? Well, yes, all of those. But what most contributes to customer engagement is how customers feel about their interactions with you and the other people at your organization. These interactions should result in customers becoming more confident, gaining a greater sense of you and your company's integrity, developing pride in doing business with you, and, if you really do your job well, developing a passion for your products and brand.

This whole notion of customer engagement is a quantum leap from many of our long-held beliefs about what good client relationships are like.

Customer Satisfaction

In the late 1970s the two buzzwords sweeping through the emerging global business community were "quality" and "customer satisfaction." Many old-line companies were taking a beating from newer rivals. U.S. car manufacturers were getting killed by the likes of Toyota and Honda. Poor quality and a lack of customer satisfaction were considered the causes for much of the drubbing.

This situation sparked intense interest in the Total Quality Management (TQM) movement and ushered in an era of increased attention to customer satisfaction. For the most part, many companies stepped up to the challenge. They were able to wring costs out of their operations as they improved their quality and customer satisfaction. By the mid-1990s we saw most industries and companies attain an 80 percent level of customer satisfaction. One of the peculiar trends we saw is that as customer satisfaction levels reach the 80 percent level, they become less valuable as a predictor of business growth.

True enough, customer *dissatisfaction* has always been a surefire way to lose business. But simply attaining a high level of customer *satisfaction* does not seem to guarantee the customer's business. This is because you and your competitor usually will have very close customer satisfaction ratings. Customer loyalty represents strength in customer relationship that extends well beyond mere *satisfaction*. To uncover the factors that build these sorts of loyal customer relationships, several of our colleagues at Gallup collected data from different industries. They looked at the factors that cause customers to stop wanting to buy products from a supplier, and the factors most likely to cause them to continue to buy.

Not surprisingly, they discovered that in most industries the number one reason customers stop buying particular products is dissatisfaction with product performance. Customers were particularly severe when they felt the company had failed to meet their most basic expectations. Those expectations are much defined by the promise the brand communicates about its product or service.

Most of us could have guessed that when a customer buys a product and it doesn't work, that customer is likely to go elsewhere. What was surprising to us was that when companies met their customers' product expectations, there was still no guarantee the customer would continue using that company as a supplier. Freedom from defects is a minimum requirement, rather than an assurance of repeat purchases. So the question is, What can assure that customers keep coming back for more?

Gallup's measure combines overall satisfaction with two other important "loyalty" components: likelihood to continue (or repurchase) and likelihood to recommend to others. When a customer provided a "top box" response in all three areas, Gallup characterized that customer as "loyal" to the product or service provider.

The research showed that products receiving high ratings for quality were more likely to obtain higher levels of repurchase, and that's not surprising. However, the effect of product quality alone often paled in comparison to the power of human interaction: Customers who felt strongly positive about their sales representatives were as much as *twelve* times more likely to continue repurchasing the product.

One of the other surprises in these data is that price in most cases was not a significant driver of repurchase intentions. While it certainly can be a factor in the original purchasing decision, companies don't develop loyal customers based on price alone. Loyal or engaged customers have an attachment that extends far beyond "getting a good deal."

In their research, our colleagues at Gallup found that in addition to questions about satisfaction and the willingness to recommend or repurchase, there was a great deal of evidence that an emotional connection or "attachment" was important. Their findings show that customer engagement is not a simple function of economics; it is personal and emotional. No wonder people play a more important role in this process than the product does.

While brand and/or product awareness, image, and

reputation contribute to building a base of customers, people are often the most powerful generators of *customer engagement*. Since Gallup researchers have found that customer engagement leads to sustainable growth and enhanced profits, those sales reps and other customer-facing employees who can generate customer engagement are worth their weight in gold!

The Engagement Effect

How do these great sales reps create customer engagement? Gallup's researchers have identified four emotional dimensions that comprise customer engagement. These dimensions begin with confidence and move on in order to integrity, pride, and passion. Together, these are the building blocks of customer engagement. Without question, high levels of customer engagement represent a tough benchmark to meet. In the various industries we studied, the number of "fully engaged" customers has ranged from the single digits (around 6 to 8 percent) to as high as 35 to 40 percent. Contrast that with the 80 percent of customers reportedly "satisfied" in these same industries.

In order to assess the level of customer engagement, our researchers first undertook a comprehensive research and development effort in which they tested a series of statements that had been used at various times to indicate the emotional "attachment" felt by a customer. The following eight statements turned out to be the best indicators of the important emotional connection between the customer and a company. Take a moment and imagine that you are one of your company's customers. Fill in your company's name in the blank and read each statement.

1. [_____] is a name I can always trust.

2. [_____] always delivers on what it promises.

3. [_____] always treats me fairly.

4. If a problem arises, I can always count on [_____] to reach a fair and satisfactory resolution.

5. I feel proud to be a [_____] customer.

6. [_____] always treats me with respect.

7. [_____] is the perfect company for people like me.

8. I can't imagine a world without [_____].

How many of your customers would strongly agree to all eight statements? You can see why high levels of customer engagement represent a very tough standard to meet, and why it's much easier to "satisfy" customers than it is to "fully engage" them.

Customers respond to these statements based on their experiences—experiences with the product (service) and experiences with people. In some businesses, such as the airline industry, customers may deal with many different people every time they purchase a ticket or fly on a plane. Every time there is contact, engagement can be affected for better or worse. In businesses in which customers deal principally with a single salesperson, however, those salespeople have enormous impact on customer engagement. So, in many industries, customers are really saying, "My *salesperson* is someone I can always trust," or "My *salesperson* always delivers on what he or she promises."

Building customer engagement is not a "sometimes" thing. Notice that the word "always" appears in five of the eight statements. That's intentional. Our research has shown that trust has to be there *all* the time or there is no trust. The same is true of respect, confidence, fair treatment, and the other practices implied by these important statements.

Consistency is clearly important in building customer engagement. Every time we have an interaction with a customer, we are either building engagement or eroding it.

Is this simply a matter of *liking* the salesperson? Don't customers really buy, as the old saying goes, from people they like? The answer to that question is a straightforward yes and no! Having your customers like you is a big advantage, but lots of customers are not looking to become best friends with salespeople. Customer engagement relates to the company and its products and services, and not only to the salesperson. Even if your customers "love" you, they still have to feel strongly engaged in what you're providing if you want some assurance that they will continue to buy.

Sometimes salespeople make the mistake of trying to be too "friendly" with their customers. Chuck told us, "Customers are different from friends. A friendship is a give-and-take relationship. There is no saying that goes 'Your friend is always right,' but every customer is all too familiar with the expression 'The customer is always right.'"

We don't mean to say that you can't be friends with your customers—you certainly can be. You might even be best friends with them, but customer engagement is different from friendship. Customers can be friendly, but they have a whole different set of expectations compared to people who are your friends just for the sake of friendship. Gallup's research into this area brings some clarity as to how these very special and unique relationships with customers are built.

Building Blocks

Gallup customer research confirms the familiar saying "People are our most important asset." Indeed, as companies seek to differentiate themselves, they must, more than ever, look to their salespeople and their other human assets in order to increase customer commitment. TQM and reengineering have squeezed defects and costs out of most organizations. Technology has increased productivity and capacity. The next competitive edge, and the sharpest, will come from employees, particularly those who face customers.

The key to winning a leading edge is in building customer attachment to you, your company, and its products and services. In the new millennium some people are afraid that salespeople will become less important. From our perspective nothing could be farther from the truth. As companies focus on customer engagement as a competitive advantage, salespeople who can create engaged customers will become even more important.

The role of a salesperson becomes clear as we examine each of the four dimensions of customer engagement:

1. **Confidence**—Customers feel that the brand or company is trustworthy and that it keeps its promises.
2. **Integrity**—Customers feel that the company treats them fairly.

3. **Pride**—Customers feel good about the product or service and also feel that using the product reflects well on them.
4. **Passion**—Now, there's a word that scares many people! What we are getting at is the strong relationship that exists between a company and a client when the latter views the former as irreplaceable.

Where, in regard to these dimensions, do you operate with your customers? How do your strengths enable you to deliver on the key components of customer engagement? How do your limitations get in the way of locking up that customer for life? Take an inventory. Think about your best practices in each of these areas. Think about how your customers would rate you and your company on each of these four levels. Think about how you can build on your strengths.

Confidence

Mike is one of his firm's best salespeople. A regional head of business development for a professional services company, Mike has become adept at leveraging his organization's reputation and the expertise of his colleagues who are charged with delivering the service. However, his organization is "administratively challenged" in Mike's estimation, and this weakness has almost cost him business on several occasions.

After his clients had complained several times about billing errors and other "dissatisfiers," Mike characteristically took matters into his own hands. He got his accounting department to agree that his administrative support person could handle accounts payable and accounts receivable for his clients.

Are your company's systems or structural challenges

causing you similar problems? Is your own inconsistent follow-through an issue?

If you don't take your clients' minds off the dissatisfiers, it's difficult to create engagement. Confidence is the foundation for the creation of customer loyalty, satisfaction, and advocacy, and that involves trust.

What makes people trust you? Different researchers have come up with different conclusions. One study says that people tend to trust people they like and are suspicious of people they don't like. Another study reports that people tend to trust people with backgrounds similar to their own. If you went to the same school or grew up in the same hometown or even have similar interests, it's easier to establish trust. A third-party introduction from someone the customer has a positive opinion of can also help establish trust. This is why referrals from existing customers can be so valuable. Making admissions about a product or company's shortcomings, and thereby "managing customer expectations," can also be a way of establishing trust.

In essence, trust is about predictability. Customers don't like surprises. They want to make sure you deliver what you promise you will deliver. If you start a relationship from scratch, the key to establishing predictability—and thereby trust—is consistency.

Nick told us that his first sales manager gave him advice that he has never forgotten and that has proved the most valuable in his career. "If you do for others what you said you would do when you said you would do it, you will set yourself apart from most of the other people in your role," recounted Nick. Having seen how true that recommendation has proved, Nick is fanatical about returning calls, sending materials when he commits to, and *never* making excuses.

Sue sells complex business-applications software. While many of her colleagues will agree to any request from prospects, she owns up to her and her products' possible limitations. "I never say that our software can do something unless I am positive that it can. If I'm unsure, I check with our systems engineers and have them demonstrate that functionality to me. I won't sell it until I see it work."

Building trust with another human being is a complicated and highly individualistic process that cannot be reduced to a simple formula. But one point every study confirms is that building trust is the very first step in developing an engaged customer!

Integrity

How we behave during the toughest times demonstrates to customers what we and our companies are *really* made of. Some advertisers new to Condé Nast publishing thought that they could get a discount on page rates during the economic downturn that struck the United States in 2000. However, as other advertisers have found for decades during other economic setbacks, Condé Nast never goes off the rate card. For the venerable publishing company, it's a question of integrity. If it had set a fair, equitable price for advertisers to reach the audiences of its publications, why would it negotiate under any circumstances?

As more companies strive to sell *value,* they risk diminishing those efforts if customers and prospects view them as inconsistent. Customers want the sense that they are being treated in an aboveboard fashion. They want transparency in pricing so that they can see the rationale for the amount you are asking. Small customers do not necessarily expect to be treated in the same way that larger customers are, but they want to *know,* rather than guess, how your discount structure works.

The words "fair" and "fairly" are important in discussions about integrity. This suggests that customers are reasonable in their expectations (most of them, anyway) and that they expect to be treated in a way that is commensurate with the terms of their business relationship with you. In effect, they want you to take their side. They want to get a sense that you are working *for* them instead of against them.

It is all too common a cliché in business that problems present opportunities, but this truism can seem less trite in light of Gallup's research. The data show that in some cases how an organization and its representatives react to problems can be a more effective developer of customer engagement than problem-free delivery. Your effectiveness in those situations seems to inspire customers to continue to do business with you.

It helps salespeople to understand what the customer thinks a fair resolution would be, to modify that expectation if necessary, and then to deliver on the new promise. Jessica put it a better way: "It's not just knowing what the customer's situation is, but rather making sure the customer knows that you know."

Pride

What kind of car do you drive? Where do you buy your clothes? What wine do you drink? Your attitude in answering those questions reveals something about the way you feel about the companies that provide those items. Are you glad to spit out your answers, or do you mumble them embarrassedly? Pride, though, is much more than snob appeal about brand image. It is more about the way we feel these companies treat us. A restaurant may have the most wonderful food in the world, but if they treat you like dirt every time you show up for a meal, you'll never become an advocate. On the other hand, a corner restaurant that knows you by name and treats you like a VIP will make you want to take your friends and colleagues there.

The companies that we do business with can become extensions of ourselves or our image. If you were buying a car, you might be imagining the admiration of your friends and neighbors when you pull into your driveway, or you might see yourself driving down a tree-lined country road with the car stereo playing your favorite song. In a business setting customers might imagine the congratulations they would get for striking a good deal, or finding exactly the right solution, or finding a great company to do business with.

These events can initiate the beginnings of pride. But this process does not end with the transaction. Maintaining or enhancing that feeling of pride as the relationship endures is what dramatically improves your chances of getting the customer to repurchase the product or to recommend a purchase to another potential customer.

When a person is proud to be a customer of a certain company, what he's really saying is, "Look what a smart choice I made." It is critical to engagement that you keep the customer feeling good about that decision.

One time we were working with a top representative of a pharmaceutical company that, despite some good products, had not become a household name. "You know," she told us as we rode with her through her territory in the South Bronx, New York, "I'm up against companies that my doctors own stock in. They like a couple of things we make, but they turn their nose up at us." Intuitively, Beth understood that to get her customers to prescribe more of her company's pharmaceuticals, she had to overcome their hesitance to be associated with her organization versus the blue-chip companies against which she competed.

As we visited doctors' offices with Beth, we were told again and again what a gem she is. It was obvious that she had aced the confidence and integrity sections of the hierarchy and that her next challenge was building pride. So, in the precious time that her busy customers afforded her, Beth was a name-dropper—the prestigious MDs who had seen great patient outcomes with her company's drugs, the researchers from the blue-chippers her company had hired, the great hospitals involved in clinical trials. It was as if in every meeting Beth were saying, "Now, Doctor, don't you want to be a part of this group?"

In many ways this pride dimension is about our customers' aspirations. All of us hear expressions from those engaged in this way all the time. "I drive a Lexus." "I stayed at the Fairmont." How quickly those aspirations can be dashed if a company does not treat proud customers respectfully. When we sense that a company or its representatives don't respect us, we feel misled and foolish for making the decision we did, in short, as if we've been taken advantage of. Proving that you respect your customers is about living up to your promise long after the sale is made. Customers want to feel that your company is as interested, or even more interested, in them as it was while the sales process was on.

What do you do to keep in meaningful contact with your customer base? How can you demonstrate that you are a partner rather than merely a vendor? Is there information you can bring to your clients? Is there an innovative way that they can use your product? Have you investigated how their needs might have changed? This kind of attention is what generates a feeling of pride in your customers.

Passion

How do you create passion? Many of the best sales representatives we have studied can sum it up in one word: discovery. They think that they can achieve this pinnacle of engagement and instill passion within their customers when they are bringing them new ways to do business. Such salespeople tell us that this is what makes them indispensable. Many look for opportunities to be innovators on their customers' behalf, rather than waiting for customer requests.

It might seem that this would be easier in technical fields, but we have seen some representatives in the most commmonplace industries become partners to their clients because of the innovations they have delivered.

Joseph is a sales rep in a smaller city for one of the nation's largest overnight shipping companies. It so happened that his largest customer in this city of 250,000 was farthest from the airport. As a result, this customer's shipments were picked up about two hours before the last customer's. In this increasingly competitive field, Joseph saw a chance to further engage his largest client. He asked the company's director of administrative services, "What would an extra two hours mean to your people preparing materials that clients had to see the next day?"

Obviously, it meant a great deal. While this routing cost Joseph's company a bit more money, it helped him create an engaged customer, one that could not imagine living without those additional two hours per day, and one that for years has resisted lower-price proposals from Joseph's competitors.

Scott is a leading "peddler of air," as he puts it, a radio advertising salesperson in one of the biggest markets of one of the industry's biggest players. Smart, diligent about follow-up, and outgoing, Scott has made a lot of friends among his customers and has inspired confidence in his clients and certainly convinced them of his and his company's integrity. But Scott is also that rare breed of salespeople who actually help customers draft and detail much of their media budgets. "Scott," some of them say, "how would *you* spend this money?" Of course, Scott doesn't put his station's call letters down on every line. He develops with his customers a sensible plan with maximum impact. "If I don't give my customers this sort of balanced advice, I'm competing with *them* rather than with the other stations in the market."

Building Loyalty

Research proves what the best salespeople have known for years: *Sales is about people.* It's not necessarily about being *liked,* but it is about being trustworthy, diligent, consultative, and, at the highest levels, inspiring.

An old scientific maxim says: "Dissecting a chicken will not tell you why it tastes good." Without question, any complicated human reaction can be difficult to portray with charts and graphs. Trying to describe how customer engagement develops can be a little like trying to describe how people fall in love. Nevertheless, our data point to some solid conclusions.

The first conclusion is that only a small percentage of many companies' customers are truly engaged. Yet increasing the number of engaged customers even by a small amount is directly linked to growing the business. Companies can no longer simply pay attention to customer *satisfaction.* Increasingly they are recognizing the importance that a strong emotional bond—one of customer *engagement*—has in building sustainable and profitable business growth.

Having high-quality products and services definitely sets the stage for developing customer engagement, particularly if customers' experiences meet the expectations that were created by the promises you communicated. But the sales force is unmistakably the biggest influence in developing customer engagement. The sales force must often keep those promises and thus has the biggest opportunity in developing customer engagement.

Not all salespeople are able to develop this emotional bond with the customer. Some simply do not have the talents necessary to interact with people in a way that will allow this to happen. Even if they are quite likable, they may never be able to move the customer to that stage of commitment—one that translates not just to the salesperson but to the company and all that it provides.

It is tempting to try to give a pat formula that you can follow to improve your own development of an engaged customer base. But like many other aspects of sales, we have not found that one exists. *What we have discovered is that your likelihood of developing engaged customers is directly tied to your own engagement and your own degree of fit.* Using your own unique talents at building relationships, gaining commitments, and thinking about customer problems will get you closer to creating engaged customers than anything else you can do.

CHAPTER 9

So, You Want to Be a Sales Manager

Sometimes a stepping-stone is just a slippery rock.

So far, this book has focused on helping you get the most out of your sales potential. By now you should have a good idea of what your strengths are and understand how to use those strengths every day in your sales efforts.

For some salespeople, there comes a time when selling is just not enough. They want the increased status, and sometimes higher salary, that comes with a promotion to sales management.

Admittedly, we have run into a few companies in which promotion to management does not seem to be the ultimate reward for solid performance in sales. An old joke goes like this:

> "Have you heard about Bill? He couldn't sell anything at all."
> "Did they fire him?"
> "No. They made him a manager!"

Nevertheless, most companies select managers from their very best salespeople. Although we would like to tell you that these career moves always work out for the best, more often they do not. Knowing the reasons for this might help you decide whether such a move is right for you. A move into management can be a great boost for some, and a land mine for others.

There is a profound difference between excellent and average managers. As you think about your future, you need to think not just about getting promoted to management, but about being an *excellent* manager. No matter what the perks and pay are, you will not find management rewarding unless you are as good or better at it than you are in your current role. Going from being a star sales performer to an average manager is a very unrewarding promotion.

Do you have the right stuff to be a great manager? What is different about those who become excellent managers and those who become only average (or, even worse, those who become absolute disasters)? To find out, we went straight to the source. We conducted in-depth interviews with more than five thousand sales managers. First, though, let's turn to a historical example to set the stage.

General Grant's Strength

When the War Between the States broke out, the North should have had an easy time of it. They had more men, more money, and more factories. What they didn't have were generals who knew how to command in battle and who loved to fight. Lincoln's generals were good peacetime leaders. They had all the necessary social graces for a refined life in Washington, but they were getting their pants kicked by General Lee.

General Grant was the exception. He was fighting battles and winning them. Grant, though, had little popularity in Washington military circles. The more refined military leaders found Grant vulgar. He had some questionable drinking habits and a checkered past (at one point he was drummed out of the military). But Lincoln recognized Grant's willingness to fight even the toughest battles and his gift for clear strategic thinking. Because of these strengths, Lincoln elevated Grant above his other military chiefs and made him general-in-chief of all Northern forces. While this displeased some Washington snoots, the tide of the war began to turn. As a result of the victories and the subsequent newspaper fame he attained, Grant became a wartime hero. After Lincoln was assassinated, the Republican Party tapped Grant to run for president of the United States. On the fame of his wartime reputation, he was carried to victory in the election.

Grant's talents enabled him to become a highly effective wartime general, but some of those same talents became his Achilles' heel when it came to being president. Many scholars view Grant's administration as one of the worst in American history. Although he had a strong desire to heal the nation after the war, he lacked the political expertise to accomplish his goal. While he was well suited for military engagements, he fumbled at diplomatic initiatives requiring tact and finesse. As a general, Grant picked superb battle commanders because he knew what he was looking for. But as president, he picked the most incompetent cabinet to ever serve in U.S. history. Even though he was personally a man of honest character, rampant corruption swirled around his presidency.

What's the moral of the story? Is it simply that a great general can make a poor president? How can a person of such obvious leadership ability be so good in one sit-

uation and an absolute failure in another? We were especially curious about this because we had observed so
many excellent salespeople turn into quite mediocre
managers. This seems to fly in the face of many conventionally held beliefs about sales and sales management. We think about these conventionally held beliefs
as success myths.

The Success Myths

These success myths generally lead us to believe that
some people are successful and others are not. Period.
For example, many people assume that if you are a success in one role or position, you are likely to achieve
success at anything else. Others maintain that successful
people have certain habits that allow them to flourish,
and that they will do well at whatever tasks they under-
take because of those habits. But our data do not support these myths. Instead, quite the opposite is often
true.

We have discovered that many people who are successful in one job show average or even poor performance in another. We have seen some great salespeople
turn into great sales managers, but we have also seen
some turn into appalling managers. What accounts for
the difference? In the course of our research, we have
found two explanations. The first has to do with the
unique strengths of the individuals, and the second has
to do with the reasons they want to become managers.
First, let's look at strengths.

Sales Management Is *Not* Sales

Many of us fail to appreciate that although some jobs might seem similar, they are really quite different. Being a basketball coach is not the same as playing on a team. Consequently, the strengths that make great players are different from the strengths that make great coaches. Being able to dunk a basketball is a tremendous advantage as a player, but it is no advantage as a coach. In the same way, sales management is not the same as selling. The strengths that make you successful as a salesperson might not help you become a great manager. Doing well in one role does not guarantee you will do well in the other.

Sometimes the very talents we rely on to make us successful in one position can become detrimental in another. That is precisely what happened in President Grant's case. His belligerent nature was ideal for fighting battles, but worked against him in dealing with political matters that required diplomacy and compromise.

Even more to the point is the example of Jeff. An extremely competitive individual, Jeff wanted to win every contest that came his way while he was a sales rep. This strong desire to be the best propelled him year after year to excellent performance. When Jeff became a manager, he drove his team to be the number one district. This all sounds very good. However, Jeff competed as a manager not only with other districts, but also with his own salespeople. He always had to be better than them. On big sales, he would take over critical parts of the presentations; he was unable to sit on the sidelines and watch. Conversations with his team members quickly turned into games of one-upmanship. Development discussions often became diatribes about how Jeff had done it better when he "carried a bag." Eventually, these types of behavior drove away Jeff's best sales reps.

Here is a key question for you to answer: Are the talents that make you successful as a sales rep likely to make you successful as a manager? There is no simple answer. But it might help to look at some additional examples.

Let's take the case of Tom. Without question, he was one of the company's top producers, surpassing the goals set for him year in and year out. One day Tom heard through the grapevine (the fastest communications medium ever invented) that another sales manager was leaving. Tom called his manager that evening to tell him that he wanted the job. Tom's manager was a bit taken aback because he was not yet aware of an opening (the manager found things out only through official company channels). Taking a deep breath, he assured Tom he would help him get the job if that was what Tom wanted. Tom told him he had thought about this long and hard, and he was sure that's what he wanted. He hadn't thought long or hard enough, as it turned out.

Tom assumed, as did his manager, that because he was one of the best sales reps in the company, he would soon become one of the best managers. But not long after Tom was promoted, his troubles began.

Tom expected his people to work around the clock, seven days a week. After all, that's what Tom did, and that's what had made him successful. Of course, in Tom's mind he was hardly a workaholic. He took plenty of time to enjoy himself. He played golf on the weekends and frequently took his wife out to restaurants. However, these golf outings and dinners always included customers. Even his vacations were taken with some of his customers. To Tom, this did not count as work.

Tom expected all of his people to take the same approach, but many objected to a 24/7 job description.
Some of his best people left because they resented his
demands. In other cases, Tom began entertaining his
sales reps' customers himself. This weakened the relationship between the customers and the sales reps, and
the sales reps resented Tom's interference.

Before long, morale in his district had sunk to an all-
time low. The sales numbers were off target. What had
worked so well for Tom when he was a salesperson was
backfiring on him as a manager. He still had the same
habits and the same strengths; what he no longer had
was the same fit.

Phil was also a top-performing representative, and,
like Tom, Phil wanted to be a sales manager. Phil,
though, had a natural interest in developing people. He
had a knack for seeing the differences among his representatives. He was careful in giving suggestions and was
especially complimentary to his best performers. In
many respects, he treated his sales reps as if he worked
for them instead of the reverse. When he communicated
with them, he made them feel as though they were the
most important people in the company, and he was
ready to listen to their complaints and respond promptly
when he could. These were the same strengths that had
built excellent relationships with his customers, but in
this case they also helped him build a great sales team.

Eventually, Phil became the president of his company.
With each promotion, he built an ever-widening core of
employees who knew he cared about them and their
growth and development.

Tom and Phil represent the two sides of what can
happen to successful salespeople when they make the
move into management. Phil's strengths worked for
him, both as a sales rep and as a manager, while Tom's
worked well only as a sales rep.

No Magic Talent

There is no single talent that great managers have and others do not. So there is no "magic bullet" we can show you. People accomplish their day-to-day tasks through a configuration of talents. We can say that the most frequent areas of differentiation we see between great salespeople and great managers are in the areas of *impacting* and *relating*. Again, the best way to illustrate the difference is through a few examples.

Troy has Command as one of his Signature Themes. As we have learned, this strength is ideal for structured sales presentations and is indicative of people who want to control the conversation. Troy is a very strong closer. When Troy presents things to his customers, he makes it impossible for them to say no.

Yet when Troy took on the role of manager, his people were uncomfortable with his "command" approach. Instead of discussing objectives, Troy would simply "sell" his sales reps on their new quotas and "close" them into accepting. His sales reps felt manipulated. These strong closing techniques were very effective for Troy as a sales representative, but they hampered his results as a manager.

On the other hand, Ted impacts people through his Developer strength. As a sales rep, Ted's interest in the personal success of his customers won him many large accounts. As a manager, he naturally became interested in bringing people along, and his strong Individualization component helped him see the uniqueness in his sales reps. Ted's salespeople felt he understood them and was interested in their growth. This has had a positive effect on Ted's sales team members and their productivity.

Both of these individuals were successful salespeople, but Ted's impacting strengths lend themselves more to a coaching role than do Troy's.

Let's look at another example in the area of relating strengths. Robert was a number one sales rep for many years. One of his Signature Themes is Harmony. He is likable and worked well with his customers. But as a manager, he was reluctant to "get tough" with poor performers. He was unable to let them know when their performance was substandard. He also did not like the challenging attitude of one of his best performers. He felt he was always haggling with him, and so he avoided contact as much as possible. Eventually, this great performer left the company. Robert's Harmony worked well for him as a sales rep, but not as a manager.

Do we mean that someone with Harmony cannot be a good manager? Not at all. But in this case, there was nothing else in Robert's Signature Themes that enabled him to deal with confrontation easily.

Jim, on the other hand, is a strong Relator. He does not meet and greet new people easily, but over time he gets to know people extremely well, especially if those people are important to him. He also has a natural tendency to invest his time in the people most valuable to him (Maximizer). These talent themes are enormously helpful to Jim and enable him to get very close to his best performers, in much the same way that he developed close relationships with his biggest customers.

Remember that no single theme makes the difference. It is the configuration of your Signature Themes that tells the story. Competition, Harmony, or Command, in combination with other themes, can result in very talented managers. Simply having Individualization or Developer or Relator as one of your Signature Themes does not guarantee success.

What Changes?

When and if you make the move from sales to sales management, the job requirements will change considerably, *but you won't*. Your Signature Themes will remain the same. After reading this book and taking StrengthsFinder, you should have a good idea of how you relate to and impact other people. Will you be able to attract and develop star performers, or will you compete with them? Are you able to sit on the sidelines and watch others "play," or will you want to grab the ball and run down the court? Perhaps you find it easy to get along with people, but can you be tough when you need to be? The answers are in your configuration of talents.

Why Manage?

Another critical question to ask yourself is, Why become a sales manager in the first place? Bear in mind that, for many managers, the daily activities of their jobs become a pain in the neck. This is because they became sales managers for the wrong reasons.

For instance, Tom wanted to be a manager because of his need for status and recognition. He has Significance as one of his Signature Themes. To him, becoming a manager was equivalent to being told he was the greatest salesperson. The promotion would effectively proclaim to his family and friends just what a good job he had done all these years. However, Tom was in for a big surprise. Being an average manager did not garner him much recognition. He received no thrill from teaching his people, from riding with them and debriefing them about their calls. He was bored. He missed the action of sales and the affirmations that would come with each closed deal. Tom had always hated paperwork, and now he had more of it than ever.

What are your reasons for wanting to become a manager? Here are some of the more common reasons we have been given by salespeople who want to move into management:

- I want more control and autonomy.
- I deserve the promotion.
- My company wants me to take the job.
- I am bored in my current job.
- I want to get promoted before they find out I really can't sell.
- "Manager" will look prestigious on my business card.
- I have been a sales rep for ten years; it's about time I did something else.
- I want to earn more money and this is the only way.
- I am tired of all the pressure to perform.
- I want people to respect me.
- Managers get nicer company cars.
- I want to spend more time in the office.
- I only went into sales so I could get into management.

These expectations frequently lead to disappointment and an unhappy career change. Why? Because they are not usually fulfilled by a career move into management. For example, take the statement "I want more control." Most managers quickly realize that they have even less control as managers than they did as salespeople. Gary's response is typical: "I thought I'd be able to call all the shots as a manager, but instead I found myself constantly boxed in between demanding reps and unyielding company policies."

Susan thought there would be less pressure on her to make her numbers. She quickly found out that she now had to worry about eight people hitting budget targets instead of simply working to hit her own. And if they were not on target, she felt all the pressure on her shoulders. "As a sales rep I would just go out and find a big order," she said, "but as a manager you can't do that nearly as easily. Not only are you behind, but there is no quick fix. I hated it."

In some companies it is possible to make more money and get a nicer company car as a manager. But if you don't enjoy what you are doing every day, those rewards will quickly become a poor trade-off. General Grant admitted that he was happier fighting the bloodiest battles of the Civil War than he was dealing with the back-stabbing diplomacy of Washington, D.C.

As you think about your reasons for wanting to be a sales manager, ask yourself: "Do I want to take on the responsibility for six, eight, or ten other human beings? Will I get a bigger kick out of watching one of my sales reps reel in a big sale than if I were doing it myself? Will I enjoy sitting back and keeping quiet on a sales call while another person makes the pitch, even if I think that I could do it much better? Do I want to explain and support company policies that I might not believe in? How will I feel when I have to fire someone, not because she is doing a 'bad' job, but because I need to recruit someone who can do a better job? Will I want to do all of the administrative work?" These are many of the day-to-day activities of sales managers. These are the realities that will impact your life far more than what is printed on your business card.

When we talk to the best sales managers about why they wanted to move into management, the list looks very different from the earlier one. They tell us things like the following:

- I enjoy developing others.
- I enjoy building a team.
- I get a kick out of helping others succeed.
- I like encouraging others to reach their objectives.
- I like working with talented people.
- I like recognizing and building what is best in other people.

These reasons are often tied to the intrinsic rewards great managers receive from their jobs. These are the reasons successful managers are willing to put up with all the travel, sacrifice, and hard work that go with being a manager. In fact, these are the reasons many great managers do not even notice the travel, sacrifice, and hard work.

It's Up to You

We have stressed two main points for you to consider. Understanding both your talents and your motives can help you decide if moving into management is a good idea for you. Don't ask yourself, "Can I be a manager?" Instead, ask yourself, "Do I have what it takes to be a highly successful manager?" Most people get satisfaction from the things they do well, and they usually do their best at things they enjoy doing.

Now, let's take another careful look at the Q^{12} items that measure productivity, profitability, growth, and retention. These items provide a "snapshot" look at the activities that great managers must do to be highly successful. Note how many of these areas can be influenced by an effective manager.

- I know what is expected of me at work.
- I have the materials and equipment I need to do my work right.

- At work I have the opportunity to do what I do best every day.
- In the last seven days I have received recognition or praise for doing good work.
- My supervisor, or someone at work, seems to care about me as a person.
- There is someone at work who encourages my development.
- At work my opinions seem to count.
- The mission or purpose of my company makes me feel that my job is important.
- My associates or fellow employees are committed to doing quality work.
- I have a best friend at work.
- In the last six months someone at work has talked to me about my progress.
- This last year I have had opportunities at work to learn and grow.

Now look at your Signature Themes. Do you see a match between your strengths and what you will need to do to meet these requirements? Can you set out expectations? Do you see the unique strengths in people, and can you encourage growth and development based on those strengths? Do you give deserved praise easily and often? Are you genuinely interested in the opinions of others, or do you just wait for them to stop talking so you can continue talking yourself? These are the kinds of questions that can help you decide if management is the right choice for you. The *best* career choice is the one that allows you to use your Signature Themes on a daily basis.

Your company might be asking you to move into management. Our data show that the need for great managers far outstrips the supply by about a four-to-one ratio. Remember, the fact that your company wants you to take the job does not automatically mean you will be a great manager. The Republican Party begged General Grant to run for office, but that did not make him a great president. In the end, moving into management is *your* decision. It's your career. It's your livelihood. It's your future. And your day-to-day job satisfaction is at stake.

Shortly after your promotion, you will be evaluated based on your results, not on how much your company wanted you to take the job. A career in management is both a journey and a destination. You need to enjoy the daily activities (the journey), but you also must produce results (the destination). In too many companies there is no path back to sales if moving into management turns out to be the wrong move. In some cases, your ego might not allow you to take a "step back," and you will find yourself stuck in a job that rewards you with little joy. This is what happens too often when someone goes from being a truly great sales rep to being only an average manager.

If all of this sounds as though we are trying to discourage you from making a move into management, we are not. But it is a crucial point in your career, and one that requires a fair amount of thought. For many it is, without question, the best move they can make. Some individuals would never be as fulfilled and as productive in their work if they chose to stay in sales.

After reading this chapter, if you think sales management is a good move for you, *do it!* If that is your decision, read on. We will reveal six suggestions from some of the word's greatest sales managers that can substantially help you on the road to success.

CHAPTER 10

Advice from the World's Best Sales Managers

It is easier, faster, and less expensive to learn from the successes of others than from our own mistakes.

So, you have decided to take the plunge into sales management after all. Don't panic if at first you feel as though you're in over your head. The change from salesperson to sales manager is often overwhelming. We have talked to many company presidents who started out their careers in sales and describe this transition as the most daunting change in their careers. "It's just such a different job," said one of those company presidents. "Suddenly a hundred demands are placed on you, and you hardly get a chance to catch your breath."

Overnight, you're faced with a mountain of paperwork, people calling and asking you to do things for them, and a thousand details that demand immediate attention. In many cases, you're behind budget and need to get things on track quickly. Well, you asked for it: Welcome to management.

Before you have time even to warm your "new manager" chair, your desk will be piled high with information. Your mailbox will be stuffed with policies and procedures, your e-mail in-box will be full, and your to-do list will seem endless. In fact, your list is endless. In the midst of this confusion, what are the most important issues to keep in mind as you try to get off to a good start?

Over several decades Gallup has interviewed some truly exceptional sales managers. Among the many things we wanted to learn from these great leaders was their suggestions for someone just embarking on the management path. We have included here advice from managers who produced the kind of outcomes that surely you want to strive for: high per-person productivity, high employee retention, highly profitable business, and great customer engagement and loyalty. You are unlikely to find advice this candid elsewhere.

Rehire Your Best

This suggestion is at the top of the list with good reason: This is your most important concern, so it should be your first priority. Your best people represent your biggest threat and your biggest opportunity.

This is what one manager observed: "I had eight sales reps in my division. The top two were responsible for more than 50 percent of the sales increases. These were two people I could not afford to lose."

But whenever there is a management change, the risk of losing good performers increases substantially. As we have already noted, the bonds between good salespeople and their managers are critical to great performance. When those bonds are broken, the likelihood of unwanted turnover increases. As a new manager, you need to reestablish that bond.

Our research leaves no doubt that a strong relationship with a manager is often the key factor that prompts people to remain with a company. The lack of such a relationship can make leaving easier. Perhaps your most important task as a new sales manager is to hang on to star performers. How? By developing the kind of relationship that builds loyalty. Your first step: Figure out who your best performers are. Your second step: Think about how they might feel about the previous manager's leaving, especially if that manager originally hired them, and then anticipate their reactions to your promotion. Your third step: Spend time with them. E-mail and voice mail are not great ways to forge a relationship; face-to-face contact is. Work with your star performers in the field and get to know them. Do this first. Do this fast. Don't assume that your best performers are best if they are left alone. They may not need your help, but they do need a relationship that bridges them to the company.

Much has been written lately about a company's culture. Gallup's research shows that culture exists at the work group level much more so than companywide. As a manager, you are responsible for establishing the culture of your sales team, for setting the tone. Therefore, you must create a culture in which star performers will thrive. When your stars came to work for your company, they did not just pick a company; they also picked a manager. Highly motivated performers often want a manager who will bring out the best in them—someone who can help them achieve their goals. So, respond to their needs. Solve their problems and get back to them quickly when they need your help. Loyalty is earned, and you must work to build it.

Mediocre managers seldom realize the role they play in retaining talent. They assume that people leave because of better offers or more exciting product lines to sell. They see themselves as bystanders in a process they cannot control. These managers simply never develop the strong relationships that help companies hold on to great employees.

Great managers, on the other hand, aren't afraid to become close with their best people. Such managers understand that strong relationships enhance productivity. While poor managers keep their distance, afraid that an employee will try to take advantage of the friendship, great managers know that relationship helps to assure that expectations for team members are clear and motivational. Without relationship, ambiguity thrives. Why does he want me to do this? Does she know how hard these goals are to achieve? Does she care? Relationship gives us the opportunity to clear the air, to sort out issues, to understand not only the "what" of our jobs—goals, rules, requirements—but also the "why."

Appreciate Uniqueness

One of our clients is a large financial institution that is, in so many ways, the best in its niche. It has mastered processes, accuracy, and cost control. The problem is, its customers don't know it. Why? The company has legislated so much of its employees' behaviors and allowed them so little autonomy that it has effectively stifled their creativity and made them slow to respond to customer requests.

One mistake many managers make, particularly new ones, is to assume that because they were successful with a certain sales style or formula, they must get everyone to sell that way. "I thought that's why they promoted me," said Keith. "After all, I was one of the best salespeople in the company. I thought if I could get everyone to sell the same way I did, they would be just as productive."

This is not a good rule of thumb. Talented people are different from one another, and this is especially true in sales. Don't expect that your best people will sell in the same way, and don't make the mistake of trying to get them to imitate your sales styles and methods. You must first understand people before you can begin to help them grow. It's easy to get off on the wrong foot with a talented representative by offering premature suggestions or advice. Your goal is to develop loyalty, not resentment.

Jerry was a successful medical device salesman. He loved his job and was always in the running for sales rep of the year. Then, the manager who hired Jerry was transferred, and Jerry's new manager, Larry, came to work with him.

All seemed to go well in the beginning. They had three spectacular days working in the field together. Nearly every account they visited purchased new products or agreed to an evaluation. After Larry left, Jerry expected to get a congratulatory letter summarizing the field visit. He had a collection of such letters from his old manager. He kept them carefully filed, and he reread them periodically in order, as he put it, to "recharge my battery." When Jerry received these letters, he would share them with his wife.

The communication he got from Larry was not one he wanted to share. Larry's note, while mentioning some of the three-day sales highlights, mainly admonished Jerry for the disorganized mess in the trunk of his company car. The manager thought that this lack of organization was no doubt responsible for Jerry's high sample budget. Larry even enclosed a trunk diagram and other suggestions for improving the situation. In disbelief and anger, Jerry ripped the note to shreds. Who in blazes did Larry think he was, criticizing him for his trunk?

A few weeks later Larry returned for another visit, and he and Jerry went straight from the airport to the biggest account in his territory. Jerry was picking up a purchase order for the biggest piece of new business ever signed in the district. As the purchasing agent (who was a pretty cranky fellow) slid the order over, Jerry looked at it for a moment and then handed it back to him. "Before I can accept this order, I feel I should tell you my trunk is a mess," Jerry said.

The purchasing agent looked confused for a moment and after an awkward silence barked, "I don't care what your @#%&@ trunk looks like," and threw the order back at Jerry. "I didn't think so," said Jerry, "but it seems to be awfully important to Larry."

Later Larry informed us that this was his most embarrassing and important moment as a new manager. "At first I was seething. All I could think of was firing Jerry when we got back to the car, but if I fired one of the best sales reps we had, the company would have rightly wanted my own head on a platter. As I began to cool down on the plane ride home, I realized that although my organizational skills had helped me to be successful, Jerry was operating from completely different strengths. What Jerry wanted and needed most was applause and recognition. Offering instruction to Jerry, at least at this point, was an insult to him. In the future I took a much different approach in managing my best people."

Excellence as a manager will not come from getting others to be like you; it will come from getting others to be more like themselves. Discovering each person's strengths and getting all their people to use those strengths every day is a secret shared by great managers. As one sales manager puts it, "You have to know them to grow them."

Lead from Strength

What's the return on your investment? We think about returns very clearly with money, but we don't often think about returns on the other resources we have at our disposal. One of the biggest resources we have is our own time. Where can you expect the best return? Great managers know the answer.

Average managers believe in the "equality myth." According to them, everyone should be treated in the same way. They bend over backwards to avoid playing favorites. Great managers view this myth for what it is—politically correct and patently unproductive.

Leading from strength means matching talent with opportunities and resources. Your job is not to divide resources equally; your job is to divide resources to produce the maximum result. Your time is one of the most important resources you have.

What produces greater results—spending time with poor performers or spending time with great performers? Too often managers believe the former. "How can I help my poor performers improve if I don't spend time with them?" some managers ask. Others argue, "I really can't teach my best people much more, so I am better off spending time with my struggling performers." It's easy to fall into this trap, and at first it can seem rewarding and productive. After all, your poor performers actually thank you for your suggestions.

But your job is to be a manager, not a professor. Often, the best performers like an audience more than an instructor. They want a witness—someone who sees them do a stellar job. Your presence brings out the best in your stars, in much the same way athletic teams play better in front of the home crowd. Your best performers need you to appreciate them and want you to applaud their great results.

If you are spending most of your time with poor performers, you will not be able to find the time to build strong relationships with your best people. You cannot build these relationships easily over the phone or via e-mail. Nothing beats face-to-face time for developing relationships. New technology is great for ease of communications, but some managers forget that these impersonal information exchanges do little to strengthen relationships.

In various studies, Gallup has observed that the attention of a talented manager will improve a salesperson's performance by about 20 percent. When the amount of attention dwindles, the salesperson's performance does too. Interestingly, managers can coax this same level of improvement from both their best and their worst salespeople. However, a 20 percent improvement from your best performers is worth much more to your company than a 20 percent improvement from an average or poor performer.

As a manager, you will *never* have enough time to go around. You must choose how and where to invest your time to yield the biggest dividends. Mediocre managers usually spend much too much time with poor and average performers. The chart on page 180 illustrates how one very successful manager allocated his time in the field with his various reps.

First of all, notice how little time this manager spends with "survivors." Often as many as one-third to one-half of the salespeople on a team might fit this description. These are salespeople with experience who have figured out how to do just enough to get by—but *only* to get by, nothing more. They aren't going to do much more, even if you spent all your time and resources on them. The only way to improve their performance is to

Performance Category	Percent of Field Time	Objective of Visit
Stars	50%	Strengthen relationship Remove obstacles Identify additional resources needed Encourage and develop
New or developing	25%	Teach Evaluate Monitor
Survivors	10%	Monitor
Poor	15%	Recruit replacements Develop key account awareness

raise the bar, and the way you do this is through your best performers.

Of course, new people need time and attention. Few training programs provide everything a new person needs to get off to the right start. New people are your next priority, after your stars.

Sometimes managers are tempted to mold a new person into a particular selling style. After all, we don't want them to develop "bad habits." But remember, selling style is a matter of strengths. Great managers don't shove a selling style down a rookie's throat. Instead, they help new people find a style that works best for them based on their strengths.

Finally, you must choose how and when to replace your worst performers. You should spend time with them to familiarize yourself with territory issues to facilitate a smooth transition once you have found an ideal replacement. If reasons preclude you from replacing a poor performer, work with him until he moves back into the survivor category. But don't let him devour your time.

The chart clearly highlights where the bulk of this manager's time is spent—with his very best people. This is where the best return on investment can be found. However, managing star performers is not always easy.

Managing the "Prima Donna"

After interviewing thousands of sales managers, we found that the biggest difference between the "great" and the "not-so-great" is the ability to manage stars. By "manage," we mean how they recruit, retain, and keep their stars producing at top levels.

We have attended countless sales award dinners. One of the most coveted awards is usually sales manager of the year, and in almost every case, that award was won because of the contribution of a star salesperson. Often, the star sold six to eight or even ten times as much as the average performers at the company.

The reason stars perform so much better than their colleagues is their incredible talent. Generally, they have striving and impacting strengths that are off the charts. Such extraordinary talents often don't make for well-roundedness, but rather for idiosyncrasies. As a rule, these unique individuals present more than their fair shares of management challenges.

We were at the annual sales banquet for a software company at which, as tradition had it, the company's top brass was honoring the year's best performers. Toward the end of the evening they introduced David as the sales representative of the year. His results were extraordinary. He had single-handedly sold more than some entire districts. The audience greeted him with a thunderous ovation as his results were recited.

Then David took the microphone and spoke. He thanked the founder of the company for the great products he had developed. He thanked the internal people for all their support. He thanked the sales manager who had hired him and taught him the ropes. He thanked his co-workers for their efforts. Each statement was greeted with an ovation. Finally, he looked out over the audience and asked each sales rep to work even harder the next year. It seemed the perfect ending to a perfect evening. Then he did the unthinkable.

Instead of sitting down and basking in his glory, he looked over the hushed audience and told them he had heard that two of the company's best products were being removed from the commission plan the following year. "I just want you to know," he said, "that if that happens, I'm leaving the company!" The audience was stunned into silence as he left the podium. The happy smiles on the executives' faces had turned quickly sour. Even though everyone agreed that he was entitled to his viewpoint, everyone also thought he had picked the worst possible time to express it.

What would you do if you were the manager? How would you handle this "star"? Is David worth keeping, or should the company get rid of him?

This particular company has a great track record of retaining star salespeople. They understand that the very best can sometimes be a bit unorthodox. The company chose to evaluate David's situation according to four criteria.

For them, performance is the first criterion. Many people can be hard to manage, but only a few can deliver the numbers year in and year out. In this company, if you want to be different, you had better be really, really good. One manager told us, "There is a fine line between a prima donna and an unemployed flake . . . and that line is productivity."

The second criterion by which the company evaluated David's action was ethics. No amount of productivity can make up for ethical lapses. Honesty and integrity are at the core of this company's value structure. They clearly understand that ethical standards must be maintained by all employees—no exceptions.

The third criterion is mission. "Mission" defines how a company wants to conduct business and the kind of reputation it wants to have. Some exclusive department stores, for example, have a certain way they want their salespeople to treat customers. So do many companies. These are not ethical standards, but they can be just as sacred to a company.

The final criterion has to do with community. How does the salesperson treat others? Some stars can be quite demanding on internal support personnel, but in this company they are not allowed to become abusive. Everyone in an organization deserves to be treated with dignity and respect. Sometimes tempers can flare and a few tense moments can erupt, but systematic "torture" of support staff is not allowed.

David's manager got together with his own boss the next morning to discuss how they should handle the situation. David was a top producer, and he had breached no ethical standards. Although his remarks had been made at a very bad time, they were actually made with a good intent and did not violate the company's standards regarding mission or community.

So they met with David and told him they had not yet made up their minds about the commission program. It was an important issue to the company because profits for certain older products were declining, and the company needed to focus its attention on newer offerings. They asked him to represent the sales force on the committee that would review this issue.

The manager never said anything about David's remarks. He realized he didn't need to. All of David's friends in the company gave him enough grief. Instead, the manager looked beyond his lapse in judgment and tried to address David's concerns and give him a way out. In this way, David could stay with the company without losing face, even if the company removed the products from the commission structure, which, incidentally, is what ultimately happened, and David eventually came to support this decision.

Handling prima donnas can be incredibly daunting. Yet your success as a manager will depend on how many of these "opportunities to manage" you can attract and retain. Everyone is different. There is no cookbook that will work for everyone.

Be a Buffer

Your role as a sales manager puts you smack in the middle between the company and the salesperson. At times even the best companies make decisions or take actions that are difficult to understand. You might find yourself disagreeing with a given strategy or decision, yet it is your role to support and sell the company's position as best you can.

Poor managers tend to fault the company rather than support a decision that makes them uncomfortable. It is often easier to blame the home office and join in the chorus of naysayers than to take on some of the ownership for an unpopular decision. Yet when you play the "blame game," you might actually be increasing the odds that one or more of your sales representatives will leave the company. The way managers accept and help their employees manage through change can help to increase loyalty to the organization. When times get tough, poor managers seem to experience an erosion of employee loyalty and engagement, while the very best managers actually enhance it.

In the same vein, you must distill all the comments you get from your salespeople and represent their concerns back to the home office. Will changing the products really help them sell more? Is the territory really getting weaker? You must filter out legitimate reasons from all too common excuses and then, as diplomatically as you can, fight for the issues that are important to your team members.

Serving as a buffer is especially important for your star performers. Simply because they are selling many times more than others are, they might need that much more support. Internal people might resent how often they call them for favors, without realizing just how much more they are selling. Sometimes stars can leave more than a few corpses in their wake after visits or calls to the home office. You might need to follow up to repair the damage.

You are the glue that will bind a good performer to the company. In many instances you will also need to be a shock absorber.

Hire the Best

When you have a vacant territory and an opportunity to recruit a new representative, follow this simple advice: Hire only the best.

Admittedly, this advice belongs in the top ten list of things that are easier said than done. Yet it is by far the most important thing you can do. Why is it so difficult?

The first reason is "glare." We might like what we see, even when we are looking at factors that have little to do with ultimate sales success. We might like a candidate's experience, and so we think she would be perfect. Or we might like something else—for example, the candidate might be very relationship driven and therefore extraordinarily likable, so we hire him. Or we might be impressed with a candidate's appearance. We call this the "Ken and Barbie Syndrome": These candidates look like they can sell, so they must be able to sell. Only later do we find out that what our new hire does best is look good.

One company we worked with wanted to hire only junior military officers who had recently left the service, assuming them to be self-disciplined individuals who could be trusted to work on their own. The company also liked the clean-cut image presented by these candidates. The company assumed it could simply teach these people how to sell to amass a perfect army of salespeople. Wrong assumption. While a few of these individuals *did* turn into great salespeople, for the most part, all the company ended up with was a clean-cut, highly disciplined, but very average sales force.

If you had to hire a comedian to entertain at an event, you would want to know the answer to one very important question: Is she funny? You don't care where she went to school or what she studied. Sales, like comedy, is very much talent based. Do your sales candidates have sales talents in abundance?

The second reason we hire average performers is time pressure. Too often we begin the recruitment process only after someone has left. This is the equivalent of grocery shopping on an empty stomach. A vacant territory produces few results, and you still have a quota to meet. Naturally, you want to get that spot filled quickly. Before long, you are ready to settle for any warm body.

The longer the territory stays open, the better each candidate appears.

The third reason for a poor hire is an overestimation of what management can do. Take a look at your business card. It says "manager," not "makeover artist." Understand the difference between what you can teach new people and what talents they need to bring to the sales role. You can teach them about your products, your industry, and your customers, but you cannot instill motivation if they do not have it. Nor can you instill impacting talents. No right-minded basketball coach would recruit twelve short people, hoping over time that he could make them taller! Similarly, even the best managers cannot make a poor candidate talented.

The fourth reason for a poor hire is that you think you can't afford the best, so you hire the best you can afford. It is true that managers often cannot hire the best in an industry because they already have jobs, they're doing great, and they're not looking to make a change. Remember, though, that you are looking for talent, not experience. Think about other sources of talent. Perhaps there are other industries in which compensation is lower but the fit is similar. Target your recruitment efforts there.

Frequently, you will have to put on your selling shoes and convince a talented person to come on board. Very often, the reason he will choose to join the company is *you*. There are plenty of bad managers out there driving great representatives out of their companies. Find one, and hire away her best.

Clearly, recruiting talent isn't easy. We know, because Gallup has been helping companies do just that for decades and has interviewed hundreds of thousands of applicants. But there remains no substitute for hiring the best. Everything else you do as a manager depends on the strengths of your salespeople. The chance to recruit talent usually doesn't come around often, so you must make the most of each opportunity. Star performers can be a bit quirky, and many an average manager is scared of hiring them. It might seem easier to play it safe with an average performer, but this strategy will never better your team.

Danny was a manager for a large, well-respected company. At one point he interviewed a thirty-nine-year-old woman for a sales position. She had no sales experience and, because of a divorce, was just entering the work world for the first time. After three interviews Danny was convinced she had tremendous sales talent. His boss strongly advised against hiring her, but Danny insisted on doing so anyway. In just a few years she was sales rep of the year. Danny looked at her talent, not her experience. But Danny was no average sales manager. He looked for the right ingredients and had the courage of his convictions.

Remember the sage advice of one of our clients: "No breath is better than bad breath" in a territory. Be patient. Hire the best. It's worth the wait.

Lots to Do

We have met few great managers who are not hard workers, and most have incredible stamina. While hard work alone will not make you great, it is tough to achieve great results without a lot of sweat equity. Still, you must carefully pick and choose how you spend your time.

It is easy to get diverted by your problem performers or your survivors. However, the story of every great manager is the story of the "stars" working for him or her. One company president summed it up this way: "You will never, I repeat, NEVER, be any better than the people working for you."

The Thirty-Four Themes of StrengthsFinder

Achiever

Your Achiever theme helps explain your drive. Achiever describes a constant need for achievement. You feel as though every day starts at zero. By the end of the day you must achieve something tangible in order to feel good about yourself. And by "every day" you mean every single day—workdays, weekends, vacations. No matter how much you may feel you deserve a day of rest, if the day passes without some form of achievement, no matter how small, you will feel dissatisfied. You have a fire burning inside you. It pushes you to do more, to achieve more. After each accomplishment is reached, the fire dwindles for a moment, but very soon it rekindles itself, forcing you toward the next accomplishment. Your relentless need for achievement might not be logical. It might not even be focused. But it will always be with you. As an Achiever you must learn to live with this whisper of discontent. It does have its benefits. It brings you the energy you need to work long hours without burning out. It is the jolt you can always count on to get you started on new tasks, new challenges. It is the power supply that causes you to set the pace and define the levels of productivity for your work group. It is the theme that keeps you moving.

ACHIEVER SOUNDS LIKE THIS:

Ted S., salesperson: "Last year I was salesperson of the year out of my company's three hundred salespeople. It felt good for a day, but sure enough, later that week it was as if it never happened. I was back at zero again. Sometimes I wish I wasn't like this because it can lead me away from a balanced life toward obsession. I used to think I could change myself, but now I know I am just wired this way. This theme is truly a double-edged sword. It helps me achieve my goals, but on the other hand, I wish I could just turn it off and on at will. But, hey, I can't. But I *can* manage it and avoid work obsession by focusing on achieving in all parts of my life, not just work."

Patti O., advertising sales representative: "I don't know how many calls I make a day, but people joke that I should have been born with a phone where one of my ears is. I go over the list of calls for the next day in my mind as I'm driving home at night. Then I write it out as soon as I walk in the door. That's my number one 'to-do' for the next day—to make it through that list. I draw little arrows next to the names of the people I know I can begin calling early. (I have to resist the urge to rewrite the list with their names on top.) When I get to the office, I just start 'dialing for dollars.' I don't stop until I've at least left messages with everyone on the list."

Ted H., customer sales representative: "I'm here every day, and I mean every day," said Ted as we pulled into one of the stores in his district. "During the week, I talk to all of my contacts in the stores. On the weekend, I just can't help myself. Those are the biggest days in a supermarket, so I just go in and make sure that all of my sections and displays look all right. My girlfriend hates it. We drive by one of my biggest stores on the way home from church. I have her go into the store with me to make the merchandise look good."

John P., account executive: "Relax? What's that? Even my vacations are busy—scuba diving, skiing, biking. I don't know how people can just sit around or lie on a beach. I'd go crazy within about five minutes."

Activator

"When can we start?" This is a recurring question in your life. You are impatient for action. You may concede that analysis has its uses or that debate and discussion can occasionally yield some valuable insights, but deep down you know that only action is real. Only action can make things happen. Only action leads to performance. Once a decision is made, you must act. Others may worry that "there are still some things we don't know," but this doesn't seem to slow you. If the decision has been made to go across town, you know that the fastest way to get there is to go stoplight to stoplight. You are not going to sit around waiting until all the lights have turned green. Besides, in your view, action and thinking are not opposites. In fact, guided by your Activator theme, you believe that action is the best device for learning. You make a decision, you take action, you look at the result, and you learn. This learning informs your next action and your next. How can you grow if you have nothing to react to? Well, you believe you can't. You must put yourself out there. You must take the next step. It is the only way to keep your thinking fresh and informed. The bottom line is this: You know you will be judged not by what you say, not by what you think, but by what you get done. This does not frighten you. It pleases you.

ACTIVATOR SOUNDS LIKE THIS:

Meghan B., sales representative: "When I was a teenager, all of my friends would ask, as soon as I showed up, 'Meg, what should we do tonight?' For some reason, I was always the one who got people rallied and moving. I now work in an electronics distribution company at which, more often than not, the internal sale is harder than the external one. We get the customer to agree to buy from us, but when we sell them on a value-added program, where the best margins are, the real sale begins. Value-adds are complicated. Once they're sold, we must secure a lot of internal resources and support to deliver on time. I think the reason I'm successful is that I have a knack for cutting through all of that. When people are hesitating or talking about all of the other deals they are working on, I get them to see why they should work on mine, why it will be good for them and the company."

Jim T., technical sales representative: "I can't sit still in meetings for very long. When people want to debate and discuss something endlessly, I get impatient. I'm okay to act if I have most of the information I need. I don't have to get all of it. I prefer action. I want to move things forward constantly. Some of my peers endlessly analyze their accounts, what they should do next, how they should do it. I believe in activity, in forward motion. Most of the time, this works. I don't mind being wrong once in a while if I can be right a lot. I can be right a lot only if I constantly try to push things ahead. The worst decision is no decision."

Fletcher B., commercial real estate broker: "During the last big downturn in our business, the brokerage started to get a little stingy with resources. An administrative person on our team had left, and the company insisted we share an administrator with another team. That just wouldn't do. We argued our case, but the regional manager held the line. So, I convinced the other team members to chip in with me to bring in a temp two or three days every week so that we could continue to grind out proposals and the other materials we needed. It worked like a charm. We continued to do well through the downturn, and we eventually won our headcount back."

Adaptability

You live in the moment. You don't see the future as a fixed destination. Instead, you see it as a place that you create out of the choices that you make right now. And so you discover your future one choice at a time. This doesn't mean that you don't have plans. You probably do. But this theme of Adaptability does enable you to respond willingly to the demands of the moment even if they pull you away from your plans. Unlike some, you don't resent sudden requests or unforeseen detours. You expect them. They are inevitable. Indeed, on some level you actually look forward to them. You are, at heart, a very flexible person who can stay productive when the demands of work are pulling you in many different directions at once.

ADAPTABILITY SOUNDS LIKE THIS:

Mike V., software sales representative: "Change creates opportunity. That's what I love about this business. I go back to the days of shared computer services. I worked with one of the largest companies in the market, but when the end-user computer revolution was dawning, I saw that the biggest money was going to be in either hardware or software. I worked with a well-respected company in mainframe computing that the world passed by. Someday that will happen to this company, and we are one of the top three in the field. It's great to be one of the first people out there, to be with the company that *creates* the market. You have to be able to apply all that you've learned elsewhere to the new game."

Bob F., investment adviser: "A couple of years ago many of my colleagues said that the Internet and online brokerage were going to make us dinosaurs. They were right, if they continued to do business the same way. I figured that I had to get myself completely out of the transaction part of our business if I was going to remain a top producer. Surely, the Internet could take transaction volume away from us, and, I thought, why shouldn't it? Why does a client who studies the market and knows what she wants to buy need to pay us a fee to do it? What I did was limit my business to fewer higher-net-worth investors. I arranged with my company not to charge them for transactions, but to enter into fee-based arrangements for managing their portfolios and working with our research staff to make the best recommendations we can. Some of these clients, of course, dabble in online brokerage, but I haven't lost any of them. I grew after online brokerage got a full head of steam in the market."

Analytical

Your Analytical theme challenges other people: "Prove it. Show me why what you are claiming is true." In the face of this kind of questioning some will find that their brilliant theories wither and die. For you, this is precisely the point. You do not necessarily want to destroy other people's ideas, but you do insist that their theories be sound. You see yourself as objective and dispassionate. You like data because they are value free. They have no agenda. Armed with data, you search for patterns and connections. You want to understand how certain patterns affect one another. How do they combine? What is their outcome? Does this outcome fit with the theory being offered or the situation being confronted? These are your questions. You peel the layers back until, gradually, the root cause or causes are revealed. Others see you as logical and rigorous. Over time they will come to you in order to expose someone's "wishful thinking" or "clumsy thinking" to your refining mind. It is hoped that your analysis is never delivered too harshly. Otherwise, others may avoid you when that "wishful thinking" is their own.

ANALYTICAL SOUNDS LIKE THIS:

Warren D., account executive in systems integration: "I'm convinced that what makes me successful in this game is that I know when to fish and when to cut bait.

Some AEs seem to fall in love with a prospect. They think that they can get a deal no matter what, and they keep believing it. I constantly ask myself, 'Is this really worth my time?' because that's all I've got. I think about the deals I've won, what those sales cycles have been like, and chart my progress with current prospects against that history. That helps me decide when it's better to fish somewhere else."

Cindy S., sales representative: "Let's face it: Sales is a numbers game. I know I need X number of prospects to close Y pieces of business. In order to have Y pieces of business, I know I have to make Z cold calls. It's that simple."

Allen H., regional sales representative: "I drive everybody crazy with questions. 'Who else will have a say in this buying decision? When do you anticipate making that decision? What is your most important consideration in making the decision? Is that factor as important to everyone on the committee? What other vendors are you considering? What has been your experience with similar products in the past? Why would you not consider using your previous supplier into the future?' For me, knowledge is power. I don't like to guess. I have to *know.* This is not something that I can easily turn off, I'll tell you. If someone tells me about a vacation, I'm liable to ask, 'How did you decide to go there? How much did it cost? Would you go back? Why? Or why not?' If a friend buys a new car, my first question is likely to be, 'How many miles does it get to the gallon?' or 'What did *Consumer Reports* say about that model?'"

Arranger

You are a conductor. When faced with a complex situation involving many factors, you enjoy managing all of the variables, aligning and realigning them until you are sure you have arranged them in the most productive configuration possible. In your mind there is nothing special about what you are doing. You are simply trying to figure out the best way to get things done. But others, lacking this theme, will be in awe of your ability. "How can you keep so many things in your head at once?" they will ask. "How can you stay so flexible, so willing to shelve well-laid plans in favor of some brand-new configuration that has just occurred to you?" But you cannot imagine behaving in any other way. You are a shining example of effective flexibility, whether you are changing travel schedules at the last minute because a better fare has popped up or mulling over just the right combination of people and resources to accomplish a new project. From the mundane to the complex, you are always looking for the perfect configuration. Of course, you are at your best in dynamic situations. Confronted with the unexpected, some complain that plans devised with such care cannot be changed, while others take refuge in the existing rules or procedures. You don't do either. Instead, you jump into the confusion, devising new options, hunting for new paths of least resistance, and figuring out new partnerships—because, after all, there might just be a better way.

ARRANGER SOUNDS LIKE THIS:

Karen R., business development manager, professional services firm: "I have this knack for taking large projects and simplifying them. I see the whole in terms of the sum of the parts. It's almost as if I can break the project down and put each of the various parts into its own little box. I think about how that would execute, how much it would cost, and see instantly how it enhances the other parts of the engagement. As a result, I've been one of the most successful people within the organization at selling very big customer engagements. This ability helps me not only with the external sale, but also with the internal execution. I help the client immediately see that this is something that *can* be done, and I make it sound simple. As I'm working this through with the client, I am mentally putting colleagues' names in appropriate boxes or parts of the engagement. Even if this is something totally new for our organization, I am instantly able to see that it can work and that it will work. I think all of that adds to the confidence with which I present."

Harry J., sales representative: "I like my job most when I have almost too many things going on at once. I'm like the performer in the circus who gets nine plates spinning on poles and runs up and down the stage tending to them. I think I'm sharpest at those times. I seem to pay attention to everything when it seems that doing so is impossible. Some people wonder how I do it. I don't know any other way."

Sarah N., district manager: "In the pharmaceuticals field, we are always staging these educational events. I've always loved them. Who should speak? Where should we hold the event? What should we serve for lunch? How will people get there? These things drive some of my peers nuts, but I love them."

Belief

If you possess a strong Belief theme, you have certain core values that are enduring. These values vary from one person to another, but ordinarily your Belief theme causes you to be family oriented, altruistic, even spiritual, and to value responsibility and high ethics—both in yourself and others. These core values affect your behavior in many ways. They give your life meaning and satisfaction; in your view, success is more than money and prestige. They provide you with direction, guiding you through the temptations and distractions of life toward a consistent set of priorities. This consistency is the foundation for all your relationships. Your friends call you dependable. "I know where you stand," they say. Your Belief makes you easy to trust. It also demands that you find work that meshes with your values. Your work must be meaningful; it must matter to you. And guided by your Belief theme, you will find that it will matter only if it gives you a chance to live out your values.

BELIEF SOUNDS LIKE THIS:

Michael K., salesperson: "The vast majority of my non-working time goes to my family and to the things we do in the community. I was on the countywide Boy Scouts board of directors. And when I was a Boy Scout, I was pack leader. When I was an Explorer, I was a junior assistant leader for the Scouts. I just like being with kids. I believe that's where the future is. And I think you can do a whole lot worse with your time than invest it in the future."

Frank P., general insurance agent: "I love what we do for families. By selling the right kind of policy to a farm owner or business owner, we make sure that that enterprise can stay in the family. One time I had this kid working for me, selling insurance to farmers. His closing rate was pretty poor. I asked him to ask his prospects permission to tape-record some of his visits with them. When I listened to the tape, I tell you, this kid was missing buying signal after buying signal. I realized he wasn't a closer, but that he had the same kind of belief in the business that I do. I played some parts of the tape over to him and said, 'When you hear people say things like that, tell them why you sell insurance.' His closing rate went way up."

Harry M., newspaper advertising representative: "I still get goose bumps when I walk into our building in the morning and see our founder's relief in bronze and our mission statement."

Michelle T., medical equipment representative: "I think I have the ability to sell everything, but I wouldn't sell just anything. I like to think that I am making a difference. That's why I love this job. Not only do we have doctors tell patients to buy our equipment for therapy, but then I often have to show those patients how to use it. I know that I'm helping those people recover and return to normal living much quicker."

Command

Command leads you to take charge. Unlike some people, you feel no discomfort with imposing your views on others. On the contrary, once your opinion is formed, you *need* to share it with others. Once your goal is set, you feel restless until you have aligned others with you. You are not frightened by confrontation; rather, you know that confrontation is the first step toward resolution. Whereas others may avoid facing up to life's unpleasantness, you feel compelled to present the facts or the truth, no matter how unpleasant it may be. You need things to be clear between people and challenge others to be clear-eyed and honest. You push them to take risks. You may even intimidate them. And while some may resent this, labeling you opinionated, they often willingly hand you the reins. People are drawn toward those who take a stance and ask them to move in a certain direction. Therefore, people will be drawn to you. You have presence. You have Command.

COMMAND SOUNDS LIKE THIS:

Zack M., account executive, systems integration: "You can't wait for your prospects to make a decision. You have to make yourself a part of their decision-making process."

Sally R., sales representative: "How do I feel when someone doubts what I've said? Angry—and I let them know it. Sometimes my big mouth gets me into trouble, but most of the time, I think it gives me the advantage in dealing with clients and moving them along."

Mike V., business development manager: "The purchasing manager at one account, in fact my largest customer, told me that since his company is spending so much money with mine, he wanted to renegotiate prices. I told him that if we were to have a pricing discussion, it would be to see how much prices should *increase* in light of all the benefits that our services have brought to his organization. That put an end to talking about negotiation."

Patti O., advertising sales representative: "I don't end any discussion with a prospect or customer without asking what my next steps should be. How can I move this toward the goal line a bit? What other information do you need to make a decision? When would be a good time to call you back? I never, not even for one second, think that the customer is in charge. I can smell the sale, and I go after it."

Paul W., business development manager: "I one time flew one of our heavy hitters to visit with a big prospect. I wanted to do everything first-class for this guy, a senior VP, so I had a limo meet us at the airport. It was evident after not very long that the driver didn't know where he was going. After yelling at him a few times about turns he'd missed, I finally told him to pull the car over. When he did, I made him give me the wheel, and I drove us to the meeting. The VP is still talking about that fifteen years later."

Communication

You like to explain, to describe, to host, to speak in public, and to write. This is your Communication theme at work. Ideas are a dry beginning. Events are static. You feel a need to bring them to life, to energize them, to make them exciting and vivid. And so you turn events into stories and practice telling them. You take the dry idea and enliven it with images and examples and metaphors. You believe that most people have a very short attention span. They are bombarded by information, but very little of it survives. You want your information—whether an idea, an event, a product's features and benefits, a discovery, or a lesson—to survive. You want to divert their attention toward you and then capture it, lock it in. This is what drives your hunt for the perfect phrase. This is what draws you toward dramatic words and powerful word combinations. This is why people like to listen to you. Your word pictures pique their interest, sharpen their world, and inspire them to act.

COMMUNICATION SOUNDS LIKE THIS:

Susan M., sales representative: "Who needs to know or would like to know? That question is always on my mind. I like to stay connected with people, and my way of doing that is by sharing information. Some of our deliverables are fairly complicated. So I always think of the four, five, or sometimes six people at the customer who should know exactly what's going on. I run through the same checklist for the internal folks I rely on. I think about how to turn these facts into a story. 'Hey, Melissa, I thought you might want to know about how those kits were coming along. I was talking to Ray, you remember, the guy in resources planning I brought over that time. Well, he was telling me . . . yada, yada, yada.' I want everyone to feel informed and comfortable. They start getting the most fidgety when they have to guess what's going on behind the scenes. I think I get beeped in the field by worried customers a lot less than my peers here."

Don T., pre-sales consultant: "One time, after a demo, a customer said to me, 'I just love all your stories,' and, you know, that's the first time it ever occurred to me that I *do* tell a lot of stories. In the course of a ninety-minute or two-hour presentation, lots of customer examples will pop into my head. I'm careful not to reveal any confidential information, but somehow these examples bring what can be pretty dry stuff to life. I mean, features and functionality. Gosh, that can get boring. I also think that when you hit a customer with something that's similar to their situation or dilemma, the benefits of our products are framed nicely for them."

Competition

Competition is rooted in comparison. When you look at the world, you are instinctively aware of other people's performance. Their performance is the ultimate yardstick. No matter how hard you tried, no matter how worthy your intentions, if you reached your goal but did not outperform your peers, the achievement feels hollow. Like all competitors, you need other people. You need to compare. If you can compare, you can compete, and if you can compete, you can win. And when you win, there is no feeling quite like it. You like measurement because it facilitates comparisons. You like other competitors because they invigorate you. You like contests because they must produce a winner. You particularly like contests in which you know you have the inside track to be the winner. Although you are gracious to your fellow competitors and even stoic in defeat, you don't compete for the fun of competing. You compete to win. Over time you will come to avoid contests in which winning seems unlikely.

COMPETITION SOUNDS LIKE THIS:

Ted H., customer sales representative: "This sign on this store should not say '[name of customer].' It should say '[name of Ted's employer],' because we own the business here. The other companies can't touch what we do in my stores."

Mark L., sales executive: "I've played sports my entire life, and I don't just play to have fun, let me put it that way. I like to engage in sports that I am going to win and not those at which I am going to lose. If I lose, I'm outwardly gracious, but inwardly infuriated."

Steven H., regional account manager: "Show me a good loser and I'll show you a loser."

Olivia Y., sales representative: "I can tell you exactly where I rank in the region and in the entire sales force every week, and I think about it every day. Right now, I'm 6 percent behind this guy John, but by the end of the quarter, I know that I'll be ahead of him. Since the end of my second year, I've never been less than number one."

Bob G., investment adviser: "I used to compete with everyone in the company until I held the number one spot for three years running. The competition was no fun anymore. I had a portfolio of accounts that would keep me in clover. So, what I started to do when I saw the other IAs was tell them how much I was making in how *few* hours. When we were younger, we would all brag about how many hours we were working."

Connectedness

Things happen for a reason. You are sure of it. You are sure of it because in your soul you know that we are all connected. Yes, we are individuals, responsible for our own judgments and in possession of our own free will, but nonetheless we are part of something larger. Some may call it the collective unconscious. Others may label it spirit or life force. But whatever your word of choice, you gain confidence from knowing that we are not isolated from one another or from the earth and the life on it. This feeling of Connectedness implies certain responsibilities. If we are all part of a larger picture, then we must not harm others because we will be harming ourselves. We must not exploit because we will be exploiting ourselves. Your awareness of these responsibilities creates your value system. You are considerate, caring, and accepting. Certain of the unity of humankind, you are a bridge builder for people of different cultures. Sensitive to the invisible hand, you can give others comfort that there is a purpose beyond our humdrum lives. The exact articles of your faith will depend on your upbringing and your culture, but your faith is strong. It sustains you and your close friends in the face of life's mysteries.

CONNECTEDNESS SOUNDS LIKE THIS:

Laura L., pharmaceutical sales representative: "I moved to a territory in the South Bronx section of New York City, known not too long ago as 'Fort Apache,' after a small town in Wisconsin. All of my friends and relatives thought I was nuts, but I love it. Most of the people my doctors serve are poor. The waiting rooms are packed. I feel so alive here, so in touch with so much of the world. The patients are from all over Latin America. The doctors are from Southeast Asia, Haiti, Trinidad, and other parts of the world. I think about the help that I'm bringing to these patients (who are on average sicker than the more affluent parts of the U.S. population) in the samples I deliver and as a result of prescriptions I convince doctors they should be writing. I'm a part of the solution."

Paul G., hotel chain account executive: "When I walk around one of our hotels, I see housekeepers, bellhops, convention services personnel, waitstaff, front-of-the-house folks, and I think, 'If I don't sell, they don't eat.' And some of them have families bigger than mine with our four kids. It makes me feel incredibly responsible, but also greatly satisfied when I land a big convention or corporate account."

Charles W., radio advertising representative: "I sell radio for lots of reasons. At first it was because I love music. Then I realized that I'm good at it and I can make a good living. Now I get my main juice from thinking about what our station does for the community. Listen to us and you'll hear good music, you'll hear from my advertisers, but you'll also hear about the importance of safe sex, about a diabetes walk, about a charity concert one of my clients is sponsoring with us to raise money for Neighborhood Watch. Now I love what I do because of what our station means to the community."

Context

You look back. You look back because that is where the answers lie. You look back to understand the present. From your vantage point the present is unstable, a confusing clamor of competing voices. It is only by casting your mind back to an earlier time, a time when the plans were being drawn up, that the present regains its stability. The earlier time was a simpler time. It was a time of blueprints. As you look back, you begin to see these blueprints emerge. You realize what the initial intentions were. These blueprints or intentions have since become so embellished that they are almost unrecognizable, but now this Context theme reveals them again. This understanding brings you confidence. No longer disoriented, you make better decisions because you sense the underlying structure. You become a better partner because you understand how your colleagues came to be who they are. And counterintuitively you become wiser about the future because you saw its seeds being sown in the past. Faced with new people and new situations, it will take you a little time to orient yourself, but you must give yourself this time. You must discipline yourself to ask the questions and allow the blueprints to emerge because no matter what the situation, if you haven't seen the blueprints, you will have less confidence in your decisions.

CONTEXT SOUNDS LIKE THIS:

Bob B., magazine advertising sales representative: "I try to see all of my accounts face-to-face once a quarter. Many of them remind me of one of my pet phrases: 'at this juncture.' Almost inevitably, that phrase comes up during one of these meetings because I like every get-together to have a bit of review, to remind accounts how they started with us or how their ads have been performing for them. I write up some notes before going in so that I can refresh them about all this. Once I talk history, I feel that I can talk about the future more confidently. So, after a few sentences of review, I guess I warn them that I'm about to ask them to make us a bigger part of their future plans when I say, 'So, at this juncture . . .' I just can't help myself. At one of our sales meetings, my peers gave me a T-shirt with that phrase on it. They couldn't stop laughing."

Sarah C., electronics OEM sales representative: "I'm part of the woodwork at this place. I know about all of the accounts since I've been around long enough to inherit so many of the good ones. Rep turnover is definitely a problem for us, and it's a big turnoff for some of our customers. The last thing they want to do is educate another rookie. They don't have to educate me, and I make sure they know it. When I visit with an account that's just landed in my lap, I sound as if I've visited the customer thirty times before. I know who called on them, for how long, and what sort of programs they bought from us."

Deliberative

You are careful. You are vigilant. You are a private person. You know that the world is an unpredictable place. Everything may seem in order, but beneath the surface you sense the many risks. Rather than denying these risks, you draw each one out into the open. Then each risk can be identified, assessed, and ultimately reduced. Thus, you are a fairly serious person who approaches life with a certain reserve. For example, you like to plan ahead so as to anticipate what might go wrong. You select your friends cautiously and keep your own counsel when the conversation turns to personal matters. You are careful not to give too much praise and recognition, lest it be misconstrued. If some people don't like you because you are not as effusive as others are, then so be it. For you, life is not a popularity contest. Life is something of a minefield. Others can run through it recklessly if they so choose, but you take a different approach. You identify the dangers, weigh their relative impact, and then place your feet deliberately. You walk with care.

DELIBERATIVE SOUNDS LIKE THIS:

Fred A., systems integration services representative: "After I do the initial prospecting and qualifying, I usually bring in a solutions engineer or solutions architect to help me and the prospect think through the prospective engagement. These engineers sometimes drive me nuts. Part of my job is to manage client expectations. When they ask for some enhancements, I will be cautious in making promises. If I do promise something, I'm sure that the customer gets a sense of how many hours it might take to build in the functionality they want. I tell the engineers to think before they answer a customer question. But some of them fall so in love with the idea of developing what the client wants that they say something like, 'Oh, yeah, we can do that. No problem.' What they don't appreciate is that I'm the one with his butt on the line when that functionality is delivered late or if it works less well than the client expected."

Paul W., business development manager: "I probably should have been an airline pilot. Everything in my life is, 'Check, check, recheck. Do I have my keys? Do I have my notes? Did I pack my ties?' I'm always prepared."

Jan M., account executive: "I don't have a wide circle of friends because I'm very cautious about who I warm up to. It takes me a while to let people in, to let them get to know me. I have to admit, while I'm making up my mind, I'm not as solicitous about them as I should be."

Developer

You see the potential in others. Very often, in fact, potential is all you see. In your view no individual is fully formed. On the contrary, each individual is a work in progress, alive with possibilities. And you are drawn toward people for this very reason. When you interact with others, your goal is to help them experience success. You look for ways to challenge them. You devise interesting experiences that can stretch them and help them grow. And all the while you are on the lookout for the signs of growth—a new behavior learned or modified, a slight improvement in a skill, a glimpse of excellence or of "flow" where previously there were only halting steps. For you these small increments—invisible to some—are clear signs of potential being realized. These signs of growth in others are your fuel. They bring you strength and satisfaction. Over time many will seek you out for help and encouragement because on some level they know that your helpfulness is both genuine and fulfilling to you.

DEVELOPER SOUNDS LIKE THIS:

Chris W., fast-tracker: "This is absolutely the best stint I've had with this company. I've been a superstar salesperson. They labeled me as a high potential, and one of the rotations the hi-po's go through is training and development. The problem is, I don't want to leave this. I love teaching, role-playing, ride-alongs. It's all of the fun I would imagine you can have as a manager without some of the headaches."

Art T., director of sales training: "I was a rep for this company for about ten years and then I was asked to teach. I've been doing that for fifteen years. It's a thrill to teach people how they can be successful, what has worked for me and other successful reps at the company. I love going to the awards banquet every year and counting off how many of the winners are my graduates."

Candace P., media representative: "Many people at our TV station used to think of me as 'Mom.' Our station manager was always asking veterans to mentor the new kids, and I always volunteered. Heck, I think I got more out of it than they did."

Ron F., book wholesaler representative: "I work an incredible number of hours but still find the time to coach soccer, softball, and basketball for girls at the junior high level, even though my daughter has moved on. When I started to do that for her, it was the first time that I'd realized how patient I could be sometimes. In most of my life I rarely find that patience, that willingness to wait for someone to get it on their own."

Discipline

Your world needs to be predictable. It needs to be ordered and planned. So you instinctively impose structure on your world. You set up routines. You focus on time lines and deadlines. You break long-term projects into a series of specific short-term plans, and you work through each plan diligently. You are not necessarily neat and clean, but you do need precision. Faced with the inherent messiness of life, you want to feel in control. The routines, the time lines, the structure, all of these help create this feeling of control. Lacking this theme of Discipline, others may sometimes resent your need for order, but there need not be conflict. You must understand that not everyone feels your urge for predictability; they have other ways of getting things done. Likewise, you can help them understand and even appreciate your need for structure. Your dislike of surprises, your impatience with errors, your routines, and your detail orientation don't need to be misinterpreted as controlling behaviors that box people in. Rather, these behaviors can be understood as your instinctive method for maintaining your progress and your productivity in the face of life's many distractions.

DISCIPLINE SOUNDS LIKE THIS:

Troy T., sales executive: "My filing system might not look that pretty, but it is very efficient. I handwrite everything because I know that no customer is going to see these files, so why waste time making them look pretty? My whole life as a salesperson is based on deadlines and follow-up. In my system, I keep track of everything so that I take responsibility not only for my deadlines but for all of my customers' and colleagues' as well. If they haven't gotten back to me by the time they promised, then they're going to receive an e-mail from me. In fact, I heard from one the other day who said, 'I may as well get back to you because I know you're going to voice-mail me if you haven't heard from me.' "

Bruce C., medical equipment representative: "How I hate loose ends! They drive me crazy. When I start something, I feel uneasy until it gets done."

Randy W., gaming industry sales representative: "I have all of my to-dos for the day on a three-by-five index card. What I didn't like about that system was, sometimes the sharp corners of the index cards catch on the shirt pocket and pull it a little out of shape. Yes, I'm a neat freak. Now, what I do: Every Sunday night I cut rounded corners with a scissors around five cards, one for each day of the workweek. It's now a perfect system for me."

Joan M., regional sales manager: "There's a system to everything I do. Someone once pointed out to me how strangely I ate M&Ms. First, I pour the contents of the bag onto a napkin. Then I put them in rows by color. Then I eat them row by row. I usually go through this process while I'm on a long conference call, so I never even realized it before."

Empathy

You can sense the emotions of those around you. You can feel what they are feeling as though their feelings are your own. Intuitively, you are able to see the world through their eyes and share their perspective. You do not necessarily agree with each person's perspective. You do not necessarily feel pity for each person's predicament—this would be sympathy, not empathy. You do not necessarily condone the choices each person makes, but you do understand. This instinctive ability to understand is powerful. You hear the unvoiced questions. You anticipate the need. Where others grapple for words, you seem to find the right words and the right tone. You help people find the right phrases to express their feelings—to themselves as well as to others. You help them give voice to their emotional lives. For all these reasons other people are drawn to you.

EMPATHY SOUNDS LIKE THIS:

Todd Z., construction management sales executive: "I have to make a lot of group presentations to executives of development companies and their financiers. I just have this knack for sensing the room, and particularly how I'm being received by the key decision makers. One time I noticed that a community relations exec was starting to glaze over. She had definitely stopped listening. As soon as possible after the group presentation, I cornered her and asked her what I could do to make her feel better about our approach to the project. She was surprised that I had noticed, but then told me about some of her concerns. She said that she had been hesitant to bring them up in the meeting because she had seen that the other influencers were with me. I certainly wanted her to feel better and certainly didn't want her knocking the deal after I had left."

Harold R., investment adviser: "Most people great at poker know that most players have 'tells,' little signs that indicate how they are really feeling about their hands. So do customers. I'm good at reading those 'tells.' They can be as obvious as the crossed arms that indicate 'I'm not listening' to more subtle indicators that you can only pick up over time. I had one customer who would flutter his eyelids a little whenever he was being, well, less than truthful. If he fluttered his eyes while saying, 'I don't have any money, Harry,' I knew he was really thinking about spending some of his money with one of my competitors. Without letting on, I played the game, but I now knew something about his hand. I provided him more information on the ways in which we were clearly differentiated from the competition to make a decision to go with them less likely. He ended the meeting by saying, 'Let me think about it,' rather than repeating that he had no more money."

Fairness

Balance is important to you. You are keenly aware of the need to treat people the same, no matter what their station in life, so you do not want to see the scales tipped too far in any one person's favor. In your view this leads to selfishness and individualism. It leads to a world where some people gain an unfair advantage because of their connections or their background or their greasing of the wheels. This is truly offensive to you. You see yourself as a guardian against it. In direct contrast to this world of special favors, you believe that people function best in a consistent environment in which the rules are clear and are applied to everyone equally. This is an environment in which people know what is expected. It is predictable and evenhanded. It is fair. Here each person has an even chance to show his or her worth.

FAIRNESS SOUNDS LIKE THIS:

Franklin H., commercial real estate broker: "Let's face it, the brokers are the rainmakers in this organization, but it's important to remember to share the credit and the applause with everyone who contributes. While I'm a team leader and get a lot of the accolades, I deflect as much of the attention to my associates as they deserve. The rookie who made the cold call, the appraiser who worked with us on the proposal, the admin who put things together so beautifully. Everyone helped, and they all deserve credit."

Nora T., account executive: "We have a rate card, and I stick to it. I think it's critical to maintain pricing integrity."

Mike V., software sales representative: "We have about as many compensation deals at our company as we have reps—it's ridiculous. Over the years lots of sales managers have found ways to get special consideration for reps they didn't want to lose, for reps who had a tough year, etc. I've been screaming about this. I think we should have transparency in the way the deals are structured. In fact, you should be able to look at someone's position and sales results and, from that, know pretty much what they took down for the year."

Focus

"Where am I headed?" you ask yourself. You ask this question every day. Guided by this theme of Focus, you need a clear destination. Lacking one, your life and your work can quickly become frustrating. And so each year, each month, and even each week you set goals. These goals then serve as your compass, helping you determine priorities and make the necessary corrections to get back on course. Your Focus is powerful because it forces you to filter; you instinctively evaluate whether or not a particular action will help you move toward your goal. Those that don't are ignored. In the end, then, your Focus forces you to be efficient. Naturally, the flip side of this is that it causes you to become impatient with delays, obstacles, and even tangents, no matter how intriguing they appear to be. This makes you an extremely valuable team member. When others start to wander down other avenues, you bring them back to the main road. Your Focus reminds everyone that if something is not helping you move toward your destination, then it is not important. And if it is not important, then it is not worth your time. You keep everyone on point.

FOCUS SOUNDS LIKE THIS:

Brad F., sales executive: "I am always sorting priorities, trying to figure out the most efficient route toward the goal so that there is very little dead time, very little wasted motion. For example, I will get multiple calls from customers who need me to call the service department for them. Rather than taking each one of these calls as they come and interrupting the priorities of the day, I group them together into one call at the end of the day and get it all done at once."

Joe P., sales representative: "I love that old motto 'He who fails to plan plans to fail.' In November or so, I think about the coming year. Where is my business going to come from? Do I have a plan for my major accounts? (I apply the 80/20 rule: Twenty percent of your clients will account for about 80 percent of your revenue.) How much business will I retain? What are the most promising prospects? I make two lists, from top to bottom—best accounts and best prospects. Let's say I have determined that 70 percent of my growth will come from existing accounts. Well, that's where I must spend about 70 percent of my time next year. That's about 170 days. I have twenty active accounts. Five of those are more than three-quarters of my business, so I will spend about 120 days with them, thinking about them, taking care of their issues and making sure that I'm positioned to be with them forever. I also know that if I don't spend 50 or 60 days prospecting for and developing new business, I'm mortgaging my future. Mapping this out keeps me from fighting fires all the time. I track my hours by activities every week to see that I'm using my time to best effect."

Futuristic

"Wouldn't it be great if . . ." You are the kind of person who loves to peer over the horizon. The future fascinates you. As if it were projected on the wall, you see in detail what the future might hold, and this detailed picture keeps pulling you forward, into tomorrow. While the exact content of the picture will depend on your other strengths and interests—a better product, a better team, a better life, or a better world—it will always be inspirational to you. You are a dreamer who sees visions of what could be and who cherishes those visions. When the present proves too frustrating and the people around you too pragmatic, you conjure up your visions of the future and they energize you. They can energize others, too. In fact, very often people look to you to describe your visions of the future. They want a picture that can raise their sights and thereby their spirits. You can paint it for them. Practice. Choose your words carefully. Make the picture as vivid as possible. People will want to latch on to the hope you bring.

FUTURISTIC SOUNDS LIKE THIS:

Irene B., customer relations representative: "My husband and I have just completed overseeing the building of a new home. The moving trucks had just pulled away, and as we walked around the place, I pointed outside and said, 'You know, we can put an addition right here someday if one of our parents wants to live with us.' He couldn't believe it. Here, this massive project was finally over, and I was thinking about what's next."

Laura L., pharmaceutical sales representative: "The FDA [Food and Drug Administration] guidelines drive me crazy, but I stick to them, of course. We're not really supposed to talk with doctors in any detail about the drugs in the R&D pipeline. That would be so cool, to be able to speculate with them about what these drugs will mean to some of their patients, what drugs they might replace. At least, though, when the drugs do come out, I'm ready to talk about them."

Frank P., general insurance agent: "One reason I've been successful is that I sell my clients a preferred future. Of course, I've been able to use my ability to talk about the future more and more as we've diversified into a broader array of financial services offerings."

Harmony

You look for areas of agreement. In your view there is little to be gained from conflict and friction, so you seek to hold them to a minimum. When you know that the people around you hold differing views, you try to find the common ground. You try to steer them away from confrontation and toward Harmony. In fact, Harmony is one of your guiding values. You can't quite believe how much time is wasted by people trying to impose their views on others. Wouldn't we all be more productive if we kept our opinions in check and instead looked for consensus and support? You believe we would, and you live by that belief. When others are sounding off about their goals, their claims, and their fervently held opinions, you hold your peace. When others strike out in a direction, you will willingly, in the service of Harmony, modify your own objectives to merge with theirs (as long as their basic values do not clash with yours). When others start to argue about their pet theory or concept, you steer clear of the debate, preferring to talk about practical, down-to-earth matters on which you can all agree. In your view we are all in the same boat, and we need this boat to get where we are going. It is a good boat. There is no need to rock it just to show that we can.

HARMONY SOUNDS LIKE THIS:

Tom H., electronics distributor sales representative: "People think that I'm so laid-back. Frankly, I get a little tired of all the salespeople we have here who feel they have to have the last word on everything. Don't they realize that people feel lousy when nobody listens to them? You don't learn while talking. By working to make people feel good and respected, I not only feel better, I learn more."

Susan M., sales representative: "More and more buys seem to involve committees or, at the very least, more than one decision maker. Some of my colleagues think about how they can appeal to the powerful folks in the group and practically ignore the others. I think about how to get *everyone* to agree to the decision and feel good about it."

Ideation

You are fascinated by ideas. What is an idea? An idea is a concept, the best explanation of the most events. You are delighted when you discover beneath the complex surface an elegantly simple concept to explain why things are the way they are. An idea is a connection. Yours is the kind of mind that is always looking for connections, and so you are intrigued when seemingly disparate phenomena can be linked by an obscure connection. An idea is a new perspective on familiar challenges. You revel in taking the world we all know and turning it around so we can view it from a strange but strangely enlightening angle. You love all these ideas because they are profound, because they are novel, because they are clarifying, because they are contrary, because they are bizarre. For all these reasons you derive a jolt of energy whenever a new idea occurs to you. Others may label you creative or original or conceptual or even smart. Perhaps you are all of these. Who can be sure? What you are sure of is that ideas are thrilling. And on most days this is enough.

IDEATION SOUNDS LIKE THIS:

Jerry G., advertising sales representative: "Ideas are sometimes the only things that keep us from being a commodity. With advertising agencies, we are selling cost per thousand [exposures]. When I can visit with the account, rather than dealing exclusively with the agency, I feel that's an opportunity to position us for better business. I came up with an idea for a how-to section on a new technology that could be sponsored by one of the biggest software providers in our readers' field. I included in the package their sponsorship of a seminar series held in major cities across the country. They snapped it up and subsequently have always thought of our publications first for their business."

George B., logistics services vice president of sales: "I heard our chairman talk about how, for a variety of reasons, our company had excess warehouse capacity all over the world. We are a global company that, among other things, designs, builds, and installs manufacturing machinery. One of my high-tech accounts a few years ago was readying for worldwide expansion. Their problem was the incredible expense involved in building a distribution network. I approached our company with the idea of selling them not only the equipment for building computers, but also some of our excess warehouse capacity worldwide. I also thought that since we are so good at transportation and logistics internationally, they might buy services in that area as well. This was a home run. It turned into a new and profitable business for our company."

Includer

"Stretch the circle wider." This is the philosophy around which you orient your life. You want to include people and make them feel part of the group. In direct contrast to those who are drawn only to exclusive groups, you actively avoid those groups that exclude others. You want to expand the group so that as many people as possible can benefit from its support. You hate the sight of someone on the outside looking in. You want to draw them in so that they can feel the warmth of the group. You are an instinctively accepting person. Regardless of race or sex or nationality or personality or faith, you cast few judgments. Judgments can hurt a person's feelings. Why do that if you don't have to? Your accepting nature does not necessarily rest on a belief that each of us is different and that one should respect these differences. Rather, it rests on your conviction that fundamentally we are all the same. We are all equally important. Thus, no one should be ignored. Each of us should be included. It is the least we all deserve.

INCLUDER SOUNDS LIKE THIS:

Claudia M., account executive: "Everything to me is 'team.' Who else should be in this meeting? Who can be helpful to us? Have we informed everyone we should? Is it time to give someone else a chance? I know that this helps me be successful. It assures that I have coverage for my customers, and it helps me extend my relationships within the company."

Nat H., sales representative: "Some people look at the inside sales reps who work on the phone all day with existing clients as the enemy or, at best, second-class citizens. Some of my peers think that the company will eventually give them the accounts we developed to save some commission dollars. That's nuts. What I've done is align myself with the two best inside reps we have. We complement one another so well. They take care of the 'farming' of accounts, while I stay positioned as the 'hunter.'"

Susan M., sales representative: "Of course, you learn so much more when you work with more and more people at the company. You get pressure not to do that. If you've teamed up successfully with someone, they expect to be your first call from then on. You should work with them again, of course, but limiting yourself can't be good, ultimately."

Individualization

Your Individualization theme leads you to be intrigued by the unique qualities of each person. You are impatient with generalizations or "types" because you don't want to obscure what is special and distinct about each person. Instead, you focus on the differences among individuals. You instinctively observe each person's style, each person's motivation, how each thinks, and how each builds relationships. You hear the one-of-a-kind stories in each person's life. This theme explains why you pick just the right birthday gifts for your friends, why you know that one person prefers praise in public and another detests it, and why you tailor your teaching style to accommodate one person's need to be shown and another's desire to "figure it out as I go." Because you are such a keen observer of other people's strengths, you can draw out the best in each person. This Individualization theme also helps you build productive teams. While some search around for the perfect team "structure" or "process," you know instinctively that the secret to great teams is casting by individual strengths so that everyone can do a lot of what they do well.

INDIVIDUALIZATION SOUNDS LIKE THIS:

Charles W., radio advertising representative: "I had a boss once who said to us over and over, 'Customers are the enemy. It's our job to beat them because they're trying to beat us.' That's wrong on so many levels. For one thing, not all customers are the same. Some certainly do want to beat you, but others are looking for partnership. I think about how different my customers are. They have different buying styles just as salespeople have different selling styles. They can be relationship driven, information driven, security driven, confident, or insecure. If you don't tailor your approach, you're leaving money out there."

Judy J., sales executive: "Sometimes I just want to react, especially when a prospect is rude or short with me. Instead, I tend to take a breath and consider where exactly they're coming from. Then I play that back to them. I convey that I care about their feelings, and that usually takes the starch out of them."

Gregory W., sales representative: "I know that I mirror the behaviors of the people I talk to. If they talk slowly, so do I. If they want to make small talk or try to get to know you before getting down to business, I take the meeting their way."

Bob F., investment adviser: "I'm a Yankee, and people told me before I moved to North Carolina that I'd never be successful down there, that you had to be a local. But, hey, all you have to do is show people that you're genuine, that you understand them, and that style will work for them."

Input

You are inquisitive. You collect things. You might collect information—words, facts, books, and quotations—or you might collect tangible objects such as butterflies, baseball cards, porcelain dolls, or sepia photographs. Whatever you collect, you collect it because it interests you. And yours is the kind of mind that finds so many things interesting. The world is exciting precisely because of its infinite variety and complexity. If you read a great deal, it is not necessarily to refine your theories but, rather, to add more information to your archives. If you like to travel, it is because each new location offers novel artifacts and facts. These can be acquired and then stored away. Why are they worth storing? At the time of storing it is often hard to say exactly when or why you might need them, but who knows when they might become useful? With all those possible uses in mind, you really don't feel comfortable throwing anything away. So you keep acquiring and compiling and filing stuff away. It's interesting. It keeps your mind fresh. And perhaps one day some of it will prove valuable.

INPUT SOUNDS LIKE THIS:

Kevin F., salesperson: "I'm amazed at some of the garbage that collects in my mind, and I love playing Jeopardy and Trivial Pursuit and anything like that. I don't mind throwing things away—material things. But I hate wasting knowledge or accumulated learning or not being able to read something fully."

Warren W., business development executive: "I like to hang around with the smartest people in my company, the engineers, the designers, the marketing folks. Sometimes I think one of those jobs might have been even better for me than sales. I also like to have them on my team, actually or virtually. I always get in on, you know, those strings of e-mails in which we debate various topics, products, processes. I feel like I'm a part of the R&D. It also makes me sound more cutting-edge when I go out into the field."

Mark B., salesperson: "I want to be able to answer most of my customers' questions or they might get the feeling that they don't need to speak to me anymore."

Intellection

You like to think. You like mental activity. You like exercising the "muscles" of your brain, stretching them in multiple directions. This need for mental activity may be focused; for example, you may be trying to solve a problem or develop an idea or understand another person's feelings. The exact focus will depend on your other strengths. On the other hand, this mental activity may very well lack focus. The theme of Intellection does not dictate what you are thinking about; it simply describes that you like to think. You are the kind of person who enjoys your time alone because it is your time for musing and reflection. You are introspective. In a sense you are your own best companion as you pose questions to yourself and try out answers to see how they sound. This introspection may lead you to a slight sense of discontent as you compare what you are actually doing with all the thoughts and ideas that your mind conceives. Or this introspection may tend toward more pragmatic matters such as the events of the day or a conversation that you plan to have later. Wherever it leads you, this mental hum is one of the constants of your life.

INTELLECTION SOUNDS LIKE THIS:

Reggie F., district sales representative: "I'm always taking time out, it seems, to get my life in order. When the weather's nice, I like to go for a walk. Sometimes I golf late on Sunday afternoon when no one is on my course and just think about everything that's going on. I wish I could find more time to do it. It's like sharpening the ax. It makes me so much more efficient."

Richard R., pre-sales consultant: "Sometimes I find myself just staring out the window with all sorts of things going through my head. I find it more relaxing than a power nap."

Jack L., investment adviser: "We live in this world that whirls around like a blender. Once in a while I just take time to catch up on the periodicals and think about what it all means in terms of what I'm going to recommend to my clients. Where is the market going? What's the cause of some of the recent developments? I have to come up with answers that feel right to me."

Learner

You love to learn. The subject matter that interests you most will be determined by your other themes and experiences, but whatever the subject, you will always be drawn to the *process* of learning. The process, more than the content or even the result, is especially exciting for you. You are energized by the steady and deliberate journey from ignorance to competence. The thrill of the first few facts, the early efforts to recite or practice what you have learned, the growing confidence of a skill mastered—this is the process that entices you. Your excitement leads you to engage in adult learning experiences—yoga or piano lessons or graduate classes. It enables you to thrive in dynamic work environments in which you are asked to take on short project assignments and are expected to learn a lot about the new subject matter in a short period of time and then move on to the next one. This Learner theme does not necessarily mean that you seek to become the subject matter expert, or that you are striving for the respect that accompanies a professional or academic credential. The outcome of the learning is less significant than the "getting there."

LEARNER SOUNDS LIKE THIS:

Sally K., manufacturer's representative: "My career has been unbelievably varied. I've sold office equipment, textbooks, and durable medical equipment. All of these had learning curves, and I enjoyed soaking up everything I could. Right now, I don't think I could tell you how a copier works, but at the time I would say what I always say, 'Hmm, that's interesting.'"

Kyle C., medical equipment salesperson: "What a nerd I can be sometimes. A couple of years ago this company was a start-up. They brought the new salespeople down to Atlanta for training. The VP of sales invited us all to go for drinks and dinner. I told him when I joined the group for dinner that I had skipped drinks because I wanted to read the materials I'd gotten that day."

Ron F., salesperson: "I never am reading fewer than three books at a time. Right now I've got a great sci-fi compilation on my nightstand. I'm reading that new Teddy Roosevelt biography in the living room. And on my commute I'm reading this history of Venice. That was one of the cities I visited with my family over the summer, and I just wanted to know more about it."

Dan P., retail salesperson: "I am part of this group of guys that gets together every month or so. We call ourselves the 'bullosophers.' We're all pretty up on current events. We all read, and when we watch TV, it's CNN. We just love to debate and argue."

Maximizer

Excellence, not average, is your measure. Taking something from below average to slightly above average requires a great deal of effort and in your opinion is not very rewarding. Transforming something strong into something superb takes just as much effort but is much more thrilling. Strengths, whether yours or someone else's, fascinate you. Like a diver after pearls, you search them out, watching for the telltale signs of strength. A glimpse of untutored excellence, rapid learning, a skill mastered without recourse to steps—all these are clues that a strength may be in play. And having found a strength, you feel compelled to nurture it, refine it, and stretch it toward excellence. You polish the pearl until it shines. This natural sorting of strengths means that others see you as discriminating. You choose to spend time with people who appreciate your particular strengths. Likewise, you are attracted to others who seem to have found and cultivated their own strengths. You tend to avoid those who want to fix you and make you well rounded. You don't want to spend your life bemoaning what you lack. Rather, you want to capitalize on the gifts with which you are blessed. It's more fun. It's more productive. And, counterintuitively, it's more demanding.

MAXIMIZER SOUNDS LIKE THIS:

Stan B., regional sales manager: "When the company asked me to take over a bad territory and build it up, at first it sounded like a great opportunity. After a while, though, it didn't feel right to me. It was like fishing in a place that had no decent fish. I put a good face on it to my boss, but I would always complain to my friends, 'There's just no business here.' I made a go of it, putting on some gains and doing a job that was considered respectable, even outstanding, by my boss, but I didn't like it. My boss fought me when I asked to be transferred to one of our biggest territories. He told me that I had found more business than anyone else had. I eventually just quit the company to accept a position with a company promising me one of the top five districts."

Karen B., sales manager: "The first thing I think about every day is my 'A' list, the big clients, the big prospects. That's where I want to put all of my energy."

Richard R., sales representative: "I realize that I'm willing to put up with an awful lot for the sake of growth. Some of my pals here like to milk a few accounts, where their friendships are. Boring! I don't mind putting up with the problems that come with the big accounts. Hey, that's why they call it 'work.'"

Positivity

You are generous with praise, quick to smile, and always on the lookout for the positive in the situation. Some call you lighthearted. Others just wish that their glass were as full as yours seems to be. But either way, people want to be around you. Their world looks better around you because your enthusiasm is contagious. Lacking your energy and optimism, some find their world drab with repetition or, worse, heavy with pressure. You seem to find a way to lighten their spirits. You inject drama into every project. You celebrate every achievement. You find ways to make everything more exciting and more vital. Some cynics may reject your energy, but you are rarely dragged down. Your Positivity won't allow it. Somehow you can't quite escape your conviction that it is good to be alive, that work can be fun, and that no matter what the setbacks, one must never lose one's sense of humor.

POSITIVITY SOUNDS LIKE THIS:

Patti O., advertising sales representative: "There's always a way. I don't see a lot of the problems and obstacles that stop other people. I just know that if I work harder, think about it more, get some help, whatever, things will work out for the best."

Edward B., telecommunications account executive: "I know so many people's birthdays, and they all get cards from me—people inside and outside the company, all of my important contacts, and, of course, my friends and relatives. I also take an hour or so out every week to write personal notes to people—e-mails, handwritten cards, you name it, just to let them know that I was thinking of them. On Super Bowl Sunday, I leave voice mails for everyone I know who is rooting for either team to congratulate them or to give them some ribbing, all in fun."

Colleen M., sales representative: "I love to surprise people. Our company makes a lot of great products, and I like bringing people the latest new product samples or the giveaways we have for promotion and special events."

Relator

Relator describes your attitude toward your relationships. In simple terms, the Relator theme pulls you toward people you already know. You do not necessarily shy away from meeting new people—in fact, you may have other themes that cause you to enjoy the thrill of turning strangers into friends—but you do derive a great deal of pleasure and strength from being around your close friends. You are comfortable with intimacy. Once the initial connection has been made, you deliberately encourage a deepening of the relationship. You want to understand their feelings, their goals, their fears, and their dreams; and you want them to understand yours. You know that this kind of closeness implies a certain amount of risk—you might be taken advantage of—but you are willing to accept that risk. For you a relationship has value only if it is genuine. And the only way to know that is to entrust yourself to the other person. The more you share with each other, the more you risk together. The more you risk together, the more each of you proves your caring is genuine. These are your steps toward real friendship, and you take them willingly.

RELATOR SOUNDS LIKE THIS:

Fletcher B., commercial real estate broker: "Many of my clients become my friends. On Saturday night my wife and I went out with the facilities manager from [name of company]. We took him out for dinner and theater. Had a blast. I've been to one of his son's high school basketball games. That's pretty typical of the way I do business. Now, there are some clients whom I don't hit it off with as well. But when I have a lot in common with a client and like to spend time with them, I look for ways to get to know them better."

Scott S., sales representative: "I'm thirty-five, my wife is thirty-two, and we just had our first baby. We were blown away by the gifts we got from my customers. And now I spend the first ten minutes of every sales call talking about our son. Some of these customers remember when I was single, remember telling me that I should settle down. It's like my extended family."

Sally C., territory manager: "I guess I don't go into any relationship with an account with expectations one way or another. I mean, I'm not out to make everyone my best buddy, but, at the same time, I don't think that I have to keep things 'professional.' Everybody gets the same Sally."

Responsibility

Your Responsibility theme forces you to take psychological ownership for anything you commit to, and whether it is large or small, you feel emotionally bound to follow it through to completion. Your good name depends on it. If for some reason you cannot deliver, you automatically start to look for ways to make it up to the other person. Apologies are not enough. Excuses and rationalizations are totally unacceptable. You will not quite be able to live with yourself until you have made restitution. This conscientiousness, this near obsession with doing things right, and your impeccable ethics, combine to create your reputation: utterly dependable.

When assigning new responsibilities, people will look to you first because they know it will get done. When people come to you for help—and they soon will—you must be selective. Your willingness to volunteer may sometimes lead you to take on more than you should.

RESPONSIBILITY SOUNDS LIKE THIS:

Nigel T., sales executive: "I used to think that there was a piece of metal in my hand and a magnet on the ceiling. I would just volunteer for everything. I have had to learn how to manage that because not only would I end up with too much on my plate, but I would also end up thinking that everything was my fault."

Sam C., sales representative: "Get it done. Those are the words I live by. I don't believe in excuses. And I don't ever wonder whose job something is. If it needs to be done for the customer, for my company, it's my job. This sometimes means staying up all night and working through weekends."

Rhonda M., account executive: "I definitely got the guilt gene. If something goes wrong, I wonder what I did, or what I could have done to prevent it. On vacations I wake up before my family does to check my e-mail and voice mail. One time I had a boss who told me, 'I could never be as hard on you as you are on yourself.' That was right! He was trying to get me to ease up a little. That's a nice problem for a boss to have."

Restorative

You love to solve problems. Whereas some are dismayed when they encounter yet another breakdown, you can be energized by it. You enjoy the challenge of analyzing the symptoms, identifying what is wrong, and finding the solution. You may prefer practical problems or conceptual ones or personal ones. You may seek out specific kinds of problems that you have met many times before and that you are confident you can fix. Or you may feel the greatest push when faced with complex and unfamiliar problems. Your exact preferences are determined by your other themes and experiences. But what is certain is that you enjoy bringing things back to life. It is a wonderful feeling to identify the undermining factor(s), eradicate them, and restore something to its true glory. Intuitively, you know that without your intervention, this thing—this machine, this technique, this person, this company—might have ceased to function. You fixed it, resuscitated it, rekindled its vitality. Phrasing it however you like, you saved it.

RESTORATIVE SOUNDS LIKE THIS:

Colby R., systems integration salesperson: "Someone once asked me, at the height of the stock market, why I didn't go into selling securities because of the money. That would never even occur to me. I mean, what we do is change a way that a company does business. In a company where we're already the primary firm, we look for ways to expand our business. This is a job of problem solving, of looking for opportunity. This is so much more interesting than peddling securities, which has to have a sameness to it after a while."

John A., consulting services account executive: "Where's their pain? That's the first thing I wonder about any prospect. Where they have pain, we have opportunity. Where they have pain, they are willing to spend money. I say to tough prospects, 'You say you don't need consultants, but, you know, you can't do brain surgery on yourself.' That suddenly makes things clear to them. They see that what we can provide is a third-party look at things, clarity about a problem that they are too close to."

Joan V., medical equipment sales representative: "If I'm really going to have leverage, I have to know how what I'm selling is better than what the doctors are using right now. So I'm always thinking about how this will make their lives better and what problems it solves or prevents for them. Then I have to think about how I am going to get them to try it, to do a clinical trial, to recommend it to the practice committee. Getting most doctors to change what they have become comfortable with is tough. I'm always noodling about these things."

Self-Assurance

Self-Assurance is similar to self-confidence. In the deepest part of you, you have faith in your strengths. You *know* that you are able—able to take risks, able to meet new challenges, able to stake claims, and, most important, able to deliver. But Self-Assurance is more than just self-confidence. Blessed with the theme of Self-Assurance, you have confidence not only in your abilities but also in your judgment. When you look at the world, you know that your perspective is unique and distinct. And because no one sees exactly what you see, you know that no one can make your decisions for you. No one can tell you what to think. They can guide.

They can suggest. But you alone have the authority to form conclusions, make decisions, and act. This authority, this final accountability for the living of your life, does not intimidate you. On the contrary, it feels natural to you. No matter what the situation, you seem to know what the right decision is. This theme lends you an aura of certainty. Unlike many, you are not easily swayed by someone else's arguments, no matter how persuasive they may be. This Self-Assurance may be quiet or loud, depending on your other themes, but it is solid. It is strong. Like the keel of a ship, it withstands many different pressures and keeps you on your course.

SELF-ASSURANCE SOUNDS LIKE THIS:

James K., salesperson: "I never second-guess myself. Whether I am buying a birthday present or a house, when I make my decision, it feels to me as if I had no choice. There was only one decision to make, and I made it. It's easy for me to sleep at night. My gut is final, loud, and very persuasive."

Harry C., account executive: "You know that saying 'Seldom right, but never in doubt'? That's me all the way, although I like to think I'm usually right, anyway. I can give you ten minutes on anything, even if I have no idea what I'm talking about."

Pat C., vice president of account development: "After I got here, I asked people what the mission statement of this place is. Well, there is none and there never has been. So I wrote a mission statement for my team. They were blown away. How did the bank feel about it? I don't know and I don't care. If they want to fire me, let 'em go ahead. I'll have three job offers tomorrow."

Ted V., salesperson: "Why do I work here? It's one of the last commission-only opportunities left. Just give me a chance to earn more based on what *I* do. Commission-only attracts the best salespeople. Every day starts at zero. You have to believe in your ability to put food on the table."

Charles C., investment adviser: "People told me that I would fail when I moved to a small town like this. 'Oh, everybody knows everybody and they only buy from people they know. Blah, blah, blah.' Well, within months I knew everybody worth knowing, and they're all buying from me. My job is to *build* relationships, not to be born into them."

Significance

You want to be very significant in the eyes of other people. In the truest sense of the word you want to be recognized. You want to be heard. You want to stand out. You want to be known. In particular, you want to be known and appreciated for the unique strengths you bring. You feel a need to be admired as credible, professional, and successful. Likewise, you want to associate with others who are credible, professional, and successful. And if they aren't, you will push them to achieve until they are. Or you will move on. An independent spirit, you want your work to be a way of life rather than a job, and in that work you want to be given free rein, the leeway to do things your way. Your yearnings feel intense to you, and you honor those yearnings. And so your life is filled with goals, achievements, or qualifications that you crave. Whatever your focus—and each person is distinct—your Significance theme will keep pulling you upward, away from the mediocre toward the exceptional. It is the theme that keeps you reaching.

SIGNIFICANCE SOUNDS LIKE THIS:

Laura L., pharmaceutical sales representative: "I like knowing that I'm a part of a doctor's therapeutic decision. I love it, after I tell them about some new research, when they give me that look that says, 'How do you know that?'"

Larry K., sales representative: "'Simply the best.' Those are the words I live by. I have to be the best salesperson at my company and the best salesperson my accounts have ever seen. I have to be associated with the best company in the field. If it's not the best, why bother?"

Mike V., software sales representative: "Do I have an engineering degree? Absolutely not. Sure, this sale is technical—eventually. But first you have to call on the highest levels of the company. Working your way down is easier than working your way up. I love calling on the big shots, the CFO, the CIO. I convince them of the payback on what we do; then I call in the technical experts from my company to deal with the bits-and-bytes types."

Peter J., sales representative: "I like the toys that come with success. You know, the his and her BMWs in the garage."

Strategic

The Strategic theme enables you to sort through the clutter and find the best route. It is not a skill that can be taught. It is a distinct way of thinking, a special perspective on the world at large. This perspective allows you to see patterns where others simply see complexity. Mindful of these patterns, you play out alternative scenarios, always asking, "What if this happened? Okay, well, what if this happened?" This recurring question helps you see around the next corner. There you can evaluate accurately the potential obstacles. Guided by where you see each path leading, you start to make selections. You discard the paths that lead nowhere. You discard the paths that lead straight into resistance. You discard the paths that lead into a fog of confusion. You cull and make selections until you arrive at the chosen path—your strategy. Armed with your strategy, you strike forward. This is your Strategic theme at work: "What if?" Select. Strike.

STRATEGIC SOUNDS LIKE THIS:

Frank B., sales executive: "It's really like a game. For every account, you map out a plan. Okay, I have to get these three people on my side. They are key. How do I do that? What if I get these two, but not that one? What's next? I know that so-and-so has a relationship with one of my competitors. How can that hurt me? What can I do about it? As I am working on a big sale, I think of all the little battles I have to win. This not only keeps me moving forward, but it also helps me feel good during the long cycles we sometimes have. I mean, sometimes I work on a deal for eighteen months before it closes."

Stan T., sales representative: "I can 'think in' with my accounts. I can turn things around, see them from their point of view. This helps me to plot out my moves three and four ahead. It's like chess."

Chris M., sales representative: "You have to have all your bases covered. I see so many people chase one big deal. Then, poof, it doesn't come through and they have nothing. You have to think about not only how to pursue an opportunity, but what opportunities to pursue. What if something doesn't come through? What else do I have? What if the bottom falls out of my biggest account, what's going to replace the revenue? You know, I drive myself crazy sometimes, but I'm never caught up short."

Bill B., sales manager: "I tell my kids that 'if' is the most important word in the English language because it makes you think. 'If I had a million dollars . . .' 'If I want to get into that school . . .' Filling in the blanks tells you your priorities."

Woo

Woo stands for "winning others over." You enjoy the challenge of meeting new people and getting them to like you. Strangers are rarely intimidating to you. On the contrary, strangers can be energizing. You are drawn to them. You want to learn their names, ask them questions, and find some area of common interest so that you can strike up a conversation and build rapport. Some people shy away from starting up conversations because they worry about running out of things to say. You don't. Not only are you rarely at a loss for words, but you actually enjoy initiating conversation with strangers because you derive satisfaction from breaking the ice and making a connection. Once that connection is made, you are quite happy to wrap it up and move on. There are new people to meet, new rooms to work, new crowds to mingle in. In your world there are no strangers, only friends you haven't met yet—lots of them.

WOO SOUNDS LIKE THIS:

Bob F., investment adviser: "Okay, you want a sure way to be successful? Get to know a lot of rich people. I belong to two country clubs because rich people belong to country clubs and you can spend four or five hours with them playing golf. There's a guy at one of them, and he's never given me a dime of business. He's had the same broker for years. He and I, though, have gotten to be friends. One day he gets sicks, so sick that he's hospitalized for a while. I go to see him. I figure that people have brought him all the flowers, candy, and magazines he needs. So I bring him fifty bucks' worth of lottery tickets. I tell him he can pass the time by scratching the numbers off. Now, he still hasn't bought a dime from me. But he's told everybody he knows what a great guy I am. And they've bought plenty."

Jill T., sales representative: "Just yesterday I find out this guy, somebody who's referred business to me, has moved back to New York. I call him to see how he did for his company while out in the Midwest. I'm always touching base and looking for excuses to stay in contact with people. Hey, you never know."

Frank B., mortgage representative: "Realtors. I know them all. When they list a house and show it for the first time, I show up to say hello to all the Realtors who show up. I stop by when they have open houses to see if they need anything. And, oh yeah, they let me leave some of my cards and materials around, too. They're my pipeline."

To keep up with Gallup's latest discoveries
in sales management, go to
http://gmj.gallup.com